Christ-Centered Conflict Resolution

Christ-Centered Conflict Resolution

A GUIDE FOR TURBULENT TIMES

Tony Merida

B&H
PUBLISHING
NASHVILLE, TENNESSEE

978-1-0877-3349-4

Published by B&H Publishing Group
Nashville, Tennessee

Dewey Decimal Classification: 303.6
Subject Heading: CONFLICT MANAGEMENT
/ GOD—WILL / RECONCILIATION

To the members of Imago Dei Church,
a joyful community of believers on mission together.
You are a joy to pastor.
I dedicate this book to you.

Acknowledgments

I'm thrilled once again to partner with my good friends at B&H. I was very honored when Devin Maddox and Ashley Gorman reached out to me with the request to write something on this particular subject, and I pray that this biblical guide on conflict resolution will help to cultivate Christ-centered peace in many people's relationships.

I wouldn't have completed this book apart from God's enabling grace and the gracious encouragement and insight of many people. I'm thankful for my bride, Kimberly Merida, for her constant encouragement. She's a true partner in ministry with me, as well as being my "dear companion" in marriage. When I see her every day, I see evidence of God's grace to me.

I'm also thankful for my sister, Amber Bowen, who encouraged me to say yes to this book, and who gave helpful feedback along the way.

I must also say thanks to my fellow staff elders Donnie Hollis and Kent Bass, who helped refine some ideas in this book. Kent, our Pastor for Counseling and Member Care, inspired several insights and ideas throughout the writing process, and contributed significantly to chapter 4. I'm also thankful for our entire elder council, a wonderful group of peacemaking pastors that serve our body so faithfully.

Finally, I'm thankful for the members of Imago Dei Church, a joyful community of believers on mission together. You are a joy to pastor. I dedicate this book to you.

> "Now may the God of peace himself
> sanctify you completely. And may your
> whole spirit, soul, and body be kept
> sound and blameless at the coming of
> our Lord Jesus Christ." (1 Thess. 5:23)

Contents

Introduction

As the 2020 Coronavirus sweeps through the globe, we currently have nine people (and two dogs) living in our house during the "stay at home" order. That's me, my wife, five kids, one house guest, and one nephew around the dinner table each night (the dogs are under the table). So when I was asked to write a book on conflict resolution, my first thought was, *Write one? I need one!*

The goal of having peaceful relationships requires biblical wisdom, prayer, and a heart filled with adoration for Jesus Christ, who has shown us reconciling love.

I hope this little book can help provide you with gospel truth and holy motivations for maintaining peace in your relationships, whether they be in your home, your neighborhood, your ministry, or otherwise. I hope that it will encourage you to seek the Spirit's help; and that it will help captivate your heart with the loveliness of the Prince of Peace, who has given us the power and pattern for how to love others.

Pastoral

Numerous Christian books on conflict resolution exist, but many are quite long and are very step-oriented. I'm not opposed to long books or to books with a lot of steps (in fact, I have benefited greatly from some of them!), but my goal here is simply to focus your attention on the grace of Jesus, as revealed in Scripture, and to apply key biblical texts to your situation.

I'm a pastor, not a professional counselor, and so I'm not delving into certain aspects of conflict resolution; nor am I treating extreme cases of abuse and law-breaking. Some issues are beyond the scope of this little book. I'm writing as if you're in my church and you're coming to me because your wife or husband or roommate or friend or coworker or kids or neighbors are driving you bananas—perhaps because you're spending more time than normal together, or perhaps because some other trial is testing your relationship. I want to give you some important passages to consider and apply.

I'm also writing with a burden that Christians be known for peace and compassion in this current hostile and tribal context in which we live. I'm writing because our faith is not a doctrine-only faith, but a doctrine-embodied faith, lived out in healthy relationships. It's truly remarkable how many passages in the New Testament speak about relationships. I told someone recently that if we invited the apostle John to preach at our church, he very well may preach something as basic as "love one another." We need to recover an emphasis on loving relationships, especially among certain groups that sadly are known for infighting, maneuvering, gossiping, and alienating people. I would love to see a reconciliation movement among Christians!

Christ-Centered

I suppose some of you picked up this book because of the "conflict resolution" part of the title, but please don't overlook the "Christ-centered" part of the title. I affirm the idea that when superior affection for Christ dominates a person's heart, it will affect one's entire life, including one's relationships.

The importance of a person's affections is not hard to illustrate because we see human beings living out of their loves/desires/affections all the time. The parent says to sixteen-year-old Rico, "Hey son, please take a shower." But he's not interested. "Rico, would you use some deodorant, please?" He's not into that either. "Hey Rico, how about some cologne? Just a little dab would do you well." Nah. "Rico, would you want to wash my car?" Forget about that idea too. Or, "Rico, you should get a job." No thanks, he would rather play video games or scroll through his social media feeds. But, remarkably, all of this changes when something miraculous happens: Rico gets a girlfriend! When he gets a new love, then you don't have to tell him to take a shower, get a job, or wash the car—he wants to. Once Rico's affections are engaged, his behavior follows. And likewise, when a person cultivates deep affections for Jesus, everything changes—use of money, time, internet browsing, and how one treats others.

When a person *wants* to honor Jesus deeply, then he will take Jesus' Word seriously, and "go and be reconciled" with his brother or sister (Matt. 5:24); when a person *treasures* the forgiveness of Jesus, she will seek to forgive "as the Lord has forgiven you" (Col. 3:13); when a person's *heart* is melted by the gentleness of Jesus, then his natural impulse will be to "gently restore" a wayward friend (Gal. 6:1; 1 Cor. 4:21; 2 Tim. 2:25).

I don't want to be simplistic and tell you that "all you need is Jesus," but I am saying that only Jesus gives us the motive, example, and power we need to "pursue peace with everyone" (Heb. 12:14). So while many conflict-resolution matters are worth our attention, Jesus must stay in the forefront of our thinking. After all, becoming like him is the goal of every Christian, including the way he makes peace with others.

To talk about the skills of conflict resolution but not focus on the heart will ultimately be a disappointing endeavor—especially in the long run. Alfred Poirier puts it like this: "Unresolved conflicts between Christians have less to do with people being skillful than with them being sinful."[1] Skills are important, but we must deal with our hearts if we are to experience peace.

Conflict as Opportunity

Though there are many ways conflict arises, I cannot help but acknowledge the particular context of COVID-19, given that my family and my church are living through it at present. When this global health crisis hit, it caused a mixed reaction in relationships. Added time together has helped some marriages and families. But others found it more difficult, as the reports of domestic abuse and divorce filing skyrocketed.[2] I'm afraid we have only seen the beginning of many relational problems connected to this experience.

So, COVID-19 pandemic or not, I'm glad you picked up this little book, as it's likely that you are either in a conflict or seeking to help someone in a conflict. If it's the former, then I want to encourage you. It's very easy to fight or to flee in a conflict. It's easy to avoid the awkward conversations that you need to have, or to lose your mind over a relational conflict in a marriage, in neighborhood feuds, in parenting, or in a church. It's easy to

---

[1] Alfred Poirier, *The Peacemaking Pastor* (Grand Rapids: Baker, 2006), 12.

[2] For one among many examples, see: Kaelan Deese, "Divorces skyrocket in China amid lockdown." Article available at https://thehill.com/homenews/news/490564-divorces-skyrocket-in-china-amid-lockdown. Accessed May 1, 2020.

avoid seeking help from a trusted friend, pastor, or counselor, and just fume or hold a grudge instead. But if you will pursue forgiveness and reconciliation in your relationships, you will grow personally, you will help others grow, and you will be doing something that not only glorifies God, but powerfully embodies his great gospel to those who need to see it with their own eyes.

Ken Sande defines conflict as "a difference in opinion or purpose that frustrates someone's goals or desires."[3] It may be impossible for you to see right now, but your conflict might be a wonderful *opportunity* to demonstrate Christ's grace, to put on vivid display what he's like and what he's done for us all. Making peace like Jesus does is not easy. It requires the Holy Spirit's enabling power. It requires us living out the fruit of the Spirit and not fulfilling the desires of the flesh. But it's worth it.

I Feel You, Parents

All five of my kids are adopted. We have a biological sibling group from Ukraine (three girls and one boy) and a son from Ethiopia. We've had our Ukrainian children for eleven years and our Ethiopian son for ten years.

All that to say, it didn't take me long to realize my need for help with pursuing peace. For the first few months, the Ukrainians spoke no English but could speak to each other. As

---

[3] Ken Sande, *The Peacemaker* (Grand Rapids: Baker, 2004), 29.

you can imagine, we had a little Cold War happening every night! They had been through a lot (as all orphans have), and there were many highs and lows early on. I remember grabbing Corlette Sande's book *The Young Peacemaker*, and working through one of the graphics inside of it. There was a spectrum, with two extremes on either side that we were trying to avoid. The left side was ESCAPE, and it included expressions of escape like "run away," "blame game," and "deny." The right side was ATTACK, and its expressions looked like "put-downs," "gossip," and "fight." The sweet spot was the middle, called WORK IT OUT, which offered a few ideas: "overlook" a minor offense, "talk" it out, or "get help" from a trusted adult who can mediate for you.[4]

All five kids now range from ages fifteen to twenty, and working through that graphic wasn't a silver bullet (maybe that's a bad analogy for a book on conflict!), but it did plant some seeds that I hope will continue to bear fruit.

Trying to be a faithful husband, parent, and pastor, all while speaking and writing and teaching, hasn't been easy. And the same is true for my wife. She wears just as many hats as me, and thorns spring up in her work, parenting, and relationship with me all of the time. Our house has known conflicts—we have blurted out the hurtful things, snapped too quickly at our

---

[4] This graphic can be found at https://rw360.org/the-young-peacemaker/, and it is originally found in Corlette Sande, *The Young Peacemaker*, 2nd edition (Wapwallopen, PA: Shepherd Press, 1997).

children, broken up the children's fights with threats, employed the cold shoulder, manipulated to get what we want, and so on. But we have also known Christ's peace—we've repented for our fleshly responses to one another, dug deep to get to the root of our frustrations, learned to appreciate each other's differences, dealt with issues directly instead of letting them simmer or drag on, and often asked forgiveness from our children when we get it wrong. Through the trials and the storms, God has been faithful. He is with us. And he is with you, Christian.

Hope for the Hurting

Jesus Christ has a miraculous ability to take an absolute mess and turn it into an amazing message. In the gospel, he shows his reconciling grace to broken people and restores them. He will not break the bruised reed, as Isaiah says (Isa. 42:3). He restores the wounded so that they can be fruitful and can flourish. The Savior is gentle, and he provides rest for the weary. I pray that as you read this book, you will experience the peace and love of Jesus in a deep way, so that it will overflow into people in your life. I pray that the Prince of Peace (Isa. 9:6; Mic. 5:5) will make you a peacemaker for the good of your relationships and to the glory of God.

CHAPTER 1

Cravings and Conflicts

The late David Powlison, a sage in the field of biblical counseling, made this statement about conflict after reflecting on some words from James, the brother of Jesus:

> I have yet to meet a couple locked in hostility (and the accompanying fear, self-pity, hurt, self-righteousness) who really understood and reckoned with their motives. James 4:1–3 teaches that cravings underlie conflicts. Why do you fight? It's not "because my wife/husband . . ."—it's because of something about you. Couples who see what rules them—cravings for affection, attention, power, vindication, control, comfort, a hassle-free life—can repent and find

God's grace made real to them, and then learn
how to make peace.[5]

Cravings underlie conflicts. This is a vitally important principle
to recognize.

My first conflict with our kids from Ukraine happened as
soon as we got on US soil. I had a lot of cravings going on inside
of me, as my wife and I had spent forty days in Ukraine, trying
to complete the adoption process and bring them home. I had the
cravings of control, praise, sleep, my comfortable home, and the
enjoyment of my favorite foods.

Speaking of food, I told the kids (through a translator) that
when we landed in the Memphis airport, I would take them
straight to a great barbeque joint. After enduring some exhaust-
ing drama on the flight across the pond, we finally made it to the
restaurant. "Pick anything you want," I told them. They made
their selections and we sat down. I prayed and then I tore into
my ribs. And then I tore into the kids—when I saw them take a
bite and then turn their nose up in disgust. I thought to myself,
*Do you have any idea what you've been eating in that Ukrainian
orphanage? Look at what I have given you! Are you this ungrateful?*

In that moment, I had all kinds of cravings ruling my heart,
and so in anger, I slammed my elbow down on the table, and

[5] David Powlison, "Powlison on Lusts of the Flesh" an interview with Justin
Taylor at https://www.thegospelcoalition.org/blogs/justin-taylor/powlison-on-
lusts-of-flesh-question-4/. Accessed April 24, 2020.

food and drinks shook and fell everywhere. The kids all looked at each other in fearful silence. I then stormed off down the concourse, praying for deliverance from evil. Once I gained my composure and had a moment with the Lord, I went back and apologized to the kids. My cravings led to this conflict. But where in the world did that craving come from? To answer this, let's press pause on James and rewind back to Genesis.

The Origin and Future of Conflict

Do you have any conflicts? If not, you will! This life is filled with conflicts—including the story I just shared about eating barbeque with my kids—because we live in a fallen world with fallen people inhabiting it.

Yet this wasn't always the case. Before the fall, there were no conflicts in the Garden of Eden. Can you imagine? As we can see in Genesis 1 and 2, there was no sin and no shame; just perfect peace. But in Genesis 3, humanity rebels against the God of Peace at the prompting of his enemy, Satan, and sin is introduced to the world, creating a rift between God and people, and also between people and each other. Sadly, as we can see in the fall, one of the primary consequences of sin is conflict.

Indeed, as a consequence for their sin, God tells the man and woman some bad news: there will be strife between them (Gen. 3:16). And in the very next chapter we see this strife being passed down generationally, as we read of one brother killing another brother (Gen. 4; 1 John 3:12). Clearly sin and conflict don't stay put; they travel down the family tree, and left unchecked, they only grow.

The good news, however, is also promised amidst the bad! God promises an answer to this problem: that One will come from the seed of the woman, One who will crush the head of the enemy (Gen. 3:15); and that victorious Savior is Jesus, the Prince of Peace.

Though strife and discord and hostility would be the way of the world after the fall, through Christ, we can overcome its effects in many ways: we can have peace with God (Col. 1:20; Rom. 5:1), we can experience the peace of God (Phil. 4:7), and by the Spirit's power we can "pursue what promotes peace" with others as we attempt to "live at peace with everyone" (Rom. 14:19; 12:18).

We pursue this peace in a conflict-ridden world as we await the new creation to come, where there will be total sha-lom. While we must deal with the grief of relational wounds, alienation, and pain now, Christians can pursue harmony with hope, for "the God of peace will soon crush Satan under your feet" (Rom. 16:20). What's more, when we do these things, we give the watching world a taste of what our heavenly home is like—peaceful and flourishing. If even ever so slightly, when we make peace in our relationships, we help the lost among us sense what a wrong world *fixed* feels like. We help them taste heaven, and remember that they were made for it. The new creation is coming, and we can help the watching world get an impression of its glory and its state of total shalom. In this way, our conflicts aren't just one-off issues we need to resolve. They have an evangelistic dimension that impacts the lost!

In short, conflict with God and others was the consequence of sin, and Jesus Christ is the answer to resolving it and securing peace for us forever. That was true in the garden, its effects will remain true in the new heavens and earth, and it's true today, in small and large conflicts alike.

You Fight and Wage War

We know the origin of conflict, we know Jesus resolves it, and we know that our heavenly future will not include it. So why is it so hard to stay at peace in the here and now? Whether it's with a spouse, coworker, neighbor, child, or friend, why do we struggle with conflict so much in our everyday lives? Let's head back into James to find out.

New Testament scholar Douglas Moo notes that the common thread running through James 3:13–4:3 is *peace*.[6] James contrasts true and false wisdom, noting that envy and selfish ambition leads to disorder, whereas true wisdom is marked by gentleness and peace:

---

[6] Douglas J. Moo, *The Letter of James* (Grand Rapids: Eerdmans, 2000), 168.

> Who among you is wise and understanding? By his good conduct he should show that his works are done in the *gentleness* that comes from wisdom. But if you have bitter envy and selfish ambition in your heart, don't boast and deny the truth. Such wisdom does not come down from above but is earthly, unspiritual, demonic. For where there is *envy and selfish ambition*, there is *disorder* and every evil practice. But the wisdom from above is first pure, then *peace-loving, gentle, compliant, full of mercy* and good fruits, unwavering, without pretense. And the fruit of righteousness is sown in *peace* by those who cultivate *peace*. (James 3:13–18, my emphasis)

It's not hard to see that James thinks Christians should be peace-loving people, living in harmony with one another, but it's also not hard to see that this is not always the case with believers! Why the disconnect between what we should be and what we are? James keeps going, probing deeper *within* us, to help us see why we have wars *among us*:

> What is the source of wars and fights *among you*? Don't they come from your passions that wage war *within you*? You desire and do not have. You murder and covet and cannot obtain. You fight and wage war. (James 4:1–2, my emphasis)

James is talking about conflicts within the community of faith, but what he says about our hearts applies to any relationship. We have wars among us because of controlling passions (what Powlison called "cravings") within us. These passions can be many things. A ruling passion could be envy or ambition. It could be selfishness (that may even be expressed in our prayers, as he says in 4:3). It might be a controlling covetous desire, or some other lust of the flesh. Regardless of the particular passion, James makes it clear that the internal war waging within a Christian eventually leads him to wage external war with others in efforts to satisfy his craving. In short, troubled people trouble people. Their internal unrest comes out on others, and creates unrest in their relationships. In the end, your relationships are usually in turmoil because *you* are in turmoil.

Do the words of James sound familiar to you? Of course they do, as James's letter has many echoes of Jesus' Sermon on the Mount—and that's seen in this passage as well. Professor Charles Quarles notes the relationship between Jesus' beatitude, "Blessed are the peacemakers, for they will be called sons of God" (Matt. 5:9) and James's instruction, saying:

> Peacemaking is the work of reconciling two alienated parties, of taking two enemies and bringing them into a relationship of unity and harmony. Only two other NT texts refer to peacemaking: Col. 1:20 and James 3:18. Colossians 1:20 [which we will consider in

chapter 3] explains that Jesus made peace between God and sinners through His death on the cross. Because of the clear relationship between the [Sermon on the Mount] and the letter of James, James 3:13–4:1 is probably more helpful in understanding the nature of peace-making in Matt. 5:9.[7]

So the importance of this passage in James for understanding the nature of peacemaking is clear.

True and False Wisdom

We all want to be wise. But when you think of a wise person, what image comes to mind? Do you think of an intellectual powerhouse? Or do you think of someone gentle and lowly—someone who deals with conflict in a humble way?

James gets at the nature of wisdom not by viewing it theoretically, as if it's some abstract concept studied by the intellectual elite, but by viewing it practically and relationally, as something *lived* by ordinary people in their everyday lives. He says that the wise person is gentle and displays godly fruit.

So how can you spot a wise person? He is the meek/gentle one. The meek person submits to God's Word and lives for God's glory. Meekness is not weakness! The meek person may well be a

---

[7] Charles Quarles, *Sermon on the Mount* (Nashville: B&H, 2011), 68.

very strong individual, but she is humble and welcoming, under control, operating with a genuine sensitivity to the Lord. You find a certain rest when you are with a gentle person because they are so full of grace. Sande says peacemakers are those who "breathe grace."[8] This doesn't mean that they are pushovers or that they avoid necessary conflict, but it does mean that they handle conflict with gentleness and humility.

Would anyone dream of coming to you for help in resolving their conflict? Would they consider you a person who has the traits of a peacemaker? Would they consider you wise—as James defines wise—to shepherd them through a conflict going on in their life? Such character flows from our union with Christ and is supercharged as we have regular and rich communion with Christ. It's in and through Christ that we live out true wisdom in a life of gentleness, and in a life of beautiful deeds toward others.

False wisdom, in contrast, is not marked by gentleness and peace but sinful cravings and quarrels. James says that "bitter envy and selfish ambition" are the source of many relational conflicts. Envy means that you want something that isn't yours, and so you get bitter about it (cf., Gal. 5:20). *Selfish ambition* is a term that is found in ancient Greek documents to speak of partisan zeal.[9] When you have a headstrong agenda for some thing or cause, and if your desires are unmet, it can lead to conflict.

---

[8] Sande, *The Peacemaker*, 11.
[9] Moo, *The Letter of James*, 133.

So the battle is in the heart. But we too often think our problems are caused by external factors. To be sure, a change in circumstances may definitely help with relational spats, but the primary problem, as mentioned previously, is that our passions are at war within us. If you have ever watched M. Night Shyamalan's film *The Village*, then you have seen an illustration of this. The people of the village attempt to shield themselves from the wickedness of society, so they create their own insulated community. But they soon find out that evil still exists within their utopian world. That's because the war is not "out there" in society, the problem is "in here" in our hearts.[10]

Or take your family vacations. Ever had a heated argument at the beach, in the mountains, on a road trip, or on a cruise ship? I call it "sanctification through vacation" as these moments (as good as they are) can often lead to moments of conflict. How about during the holidays? Why are these times often hard? Might it be that James is correct? Our cravings for a hassle-free life, for well-behaved kids, for worldly success, for comfort and rest, go unmet, and we get angry about it.

Now, not all conflicts come from bad motives. It's not wrong to want to rest, or to have well-behaved kids, or to do well in your vocation. Sometimes, disagreements exist because of a difference

---

[10] I'm indebted to Stan Norman for this illustration found in Daniel L. Akin, ed., *A Theology for the Church*. Revised edition (Nashville: B&H, 2014), 337.

in values, goals, or giftings in the pursuit of something.[11] This may lead to anger and arguing, but it doesn't have to. Sometimes a conflict may come from poor communication, or from the challenge of having limited resources.[12] Other times, a needed conflict arises on a societal level as a way to signal that something very wrong has happened and needs to be righted. These kinds of challenges can be opportunities to grow, show grace, and seek justice.

But often our conflicts arise from a ruling desire in our heart. Dr. Robert Jones gives a helpful list of questions to ask for detecting an "inordinate desire."

- Does it consume you? Do you dwell on it continually?
- Are you willing to sin to get it?
- Do you sin when you don't get it?[13]

These may be hard questions to ask yourself, but it's a gift for your sin to be exposed. Often conflicts expose these idols, and this gives us the opportunity to repent and experience renewal and spiritual growth (cf., James 4:4–10).

There's one more important detail that we cannot overlook when we consider this battle: the devil. Did you notice that James says that this false wisdom is "earthly, unspiritual and

---

[11] Sande, *The Peacemaker*, 30.

[12] Ibid.

[13] Robert D. Jones, *Uprooting Anger* (Phillipsburg, NJ: P&R, 2005), 56.

demonic" (James 3:15, my emphasis; cf., 4:7)? True wisdom comes from above—it's a gift from God. False wisdom comes from below—from the world, the flesh and the devil. Sinful anger, self-centeredness, manipulation, unchecked obsession for control, abuse, and so on, all come from below.

Have you ever considered the fact that there is spiritual warfare involved in your relationships? Sure, the devil is influencing those engaged in evil on a large scale, as in human trafficking, terrorist attacks, and political corruption. But the devil is also out to ravage friendships and marriages, which is why we often see the devil mentioned in reference to relationships (Eph. 4:27; 1 Tim. 3:6–7).

A few years ago, I was having a relational conflict with another Christian leader. There had been no heated arguments, nor anything done in public, but things weren't what they used to be. This grieved me. Despite having some awkward conversations with each other, I still sensed the presence of warfare. I told a friend of mine, "I text him periodically just to keep the devil out of our friendship." I really did feel as if the things that led to our lack of harmony, and the unsettledness that I was facing, was a result of warfare. So I decided frequent and edifying communication would be a way of dealing with the devil. Maintaining peace in relationships sometimes requires us not only to defend our relationships against the enemy's attacks when the situation has already become dire, but to go on the offensive, making preemptive attempts to secure peace before the devil gets to our door. Peacemaking is spiritual warfare, and it requires the Spirit's power.

Qualities of Peacemakers

James's description of the qualities produced by wisdom from above (James 3:17–18) resembles Paul's list in the classic "fruit of the Spirit" passage (which we will consider in the next chapter).

The first word *pure* denotes innocence or blamelessness (James 3:17). The seven qualities then mentioned are specific dimensions of this purity.[14] Recall also that there is an important beatitude that precedes Jesus' words on being a peacemaker: "Blessed are the pure in heart, for they will see God" (Matt. 5:8). You have to be pure in heart before you can ever be a peacemaker, and that purity comes through Jesus Christ, the pure one who cleanses sinners, whom we will see, and who will purify all things, produces in us a desire for living a pure life. What does this lifestyle look like? We can put James's peacemaking list in three groups.

Group 1: *Peace-Loving, Gentle, and Compliant.* *Peace-loving* is especially important, as it heads the list of specific virtues, and is picked up again in verse 18. Each of us pursues what we love; we won't pursue peace with others if we don't *love* it to begin with. So how do we spot a peace-lover? The peace-loving

---

[14] Moo, *The Letter of James*, 175.

person speaks with grace, isn't easily angered, seeks reconciliation and overlooks minor offenses. The Old Testament often connects *wisdom* with peace: "Her ways [the way of wisdom] are ways of pleasantness, and all her paths are peace" (Prov. 3:17 ESV). Instead of resolving a conflict with brute force like the world does, James says being *gentle* and *compliant* (or "open to reason," ESV) is the godly way to pursue peace. Gentleness is emphasized throughout Scripture, and often in the context of admonitions on conflict and quarreling (cf., 2 Tim. 2:14–26; Titus 3:2). Being open to reason or "compliant" means to defer when appropriate; it means to be willing to get along with others.

Group 2: *Full of Mercy and Good Fruits.* Jesus spoke often of the importance of showing mercy (Matt. 5:7; 18:21–35; 23:23; Luke 10:37). James emphasized it previously in chapter 2, as he talked about the royal law of neighbor love (2:8–13). Now he links it with good fruit. Being a merciful person is a real sign of the fruit of the gospel in our lives. Those who know the depth of God's saving mercy (Eph. 2:4), are mercy-showers. Imagine how many conflicts in our lives might subside if we simply showed more mercy to one another!

Group 3: *Unwavering and Without Pretense.* *Unwavering* is only used here in the New Testament. And there's some difficulty in translating it. It carries the idea of either "undoubting," in the sense of "simple" or "straightforward." Or for being "undivided"—that is, in loyalty to God. The CSB translates it "unwavering" as James probably has in mind something like being "undivided" and not double-minded. This also fits with the next word that means "without pretense." It means "not playing a part"—being real. The wise person is stable, trustworthy, and transparent. Again, can you imagine how conflict in this world might look different if all parties in any given disagreement were like this?

These are the fruits of true wisdom. What a contrast with self-ambition, envy, and jealousy!

Cultivating Peace

In the final verse of James 3, the inspired writer returns to what seems to be the big concern: peace in the fellowship. He gives a proverbial statement: "And the fruit of righteousness is sown in peace by those who cultivate peace" (3:18). Righteousness here is practical righteousness; it means that which pleases God (cf., James 1:20). God made us to flourish in a context of peace. When people aren't full of selfish ambition and envy, but are in harmony, great fruits of righteousness are displayed.

Our responsibility is to work to "cultivate peace" so that righteousness will be produced. The seventh beatitude ("blessed are the peacemakers") introduces a theme that Jesus expands in the Sermon on the Mount. Jesus' words explain all that cultivating peace means for us. First, our Lord commands that we should interrupt worship in order to seek reconciliation with a fellow disciple whom we have offended (Matt. 5:21–26). Next, he commands us to refrain from retaliating against those who hurt us (vv. 38–41). Jesus then directs us to love our enemies and pray *for*, not against, our persecutors (vv. 43–48). And he doesn't stop in chapter 5! In Matthew 6, Jesus magnifies the importance of forgiving others in the Lord's Prayer (Matt. 6:14). And still, he's not done. Finally, in chapter 7, he commands us to "get the log out of our eye" before noticing the speck in our brother's eye (Matt. 7:1–5).

Clearly being a peacemaker is a big deal to Jesus! This way of life marks the citizens of his kingdom (cf., Mark 9:50). Quarles states, "The ministry of peacemaking involved putting an end to conflict by refusing to postpone apologies or restitution, refusing to seek revenge, humbly serving one's enemies, and having a love for others that is stronger than their hatred."[15]

Have you postponed an apology? Are you out for revenge? Are you loving your enemies? Do you need to forgive someone? Do you need to face up to your own failures before detecting another person's failures? By God's grace, let's live by Christ's words!

There's great blessing for peacemakers: "for they will be called sons of God" (Matt. 5:9). Christians have a unique relationship with God because of the reconciling work of Jesus, as we are made sons and daughters of God now. And God calls his sons and daughters *peacemakers*. Further, most of the promises in

---

[15] Quarles, *Sermon on the Mount*, 69.

the Beatitudes have an end time view, so the promise here refers to judgment in which Jesus will separate his enemies from his children, calling his followers "sons of God," who will enjoy a glorious inheritance.

Jesus, the Prince of Peace, has brought us peace with God. He has called us to be peacemakers now. And we do this work by God's grace until Jesus makes all things new, ushering in total shalom, where the lion will dwell with the lamb in perfect harmony. Let's seek to "bring this future into the present" as we pursue peace in our relationships to the glory of God. Let's show the world what kind of King we have and what kind of kingdom we belong to.

CHAPTER 2

Making Peace by the Blood of the Cross

Maybe you've seen the baseball movie *The Sandlot,* where the new kid on the block (Smalls) is trying to be accepted by the neighborhood boys. His buddies need a baseball, so he takes one from his dad's bedroom. What he fails to realize (because he knows nothing about baseball) is that he grabbed an autographed ball signed by Babe Ruth! His pals ask, "Where did you get that ball?" And this classic exchange happens:

> **Smalls:** I don't know. Some lady gave it to him. She even signed her name on it . . . Ruth. Baby Ruth.
>
> **All:** BABE RUTH?! [Everyone screams in horror and rushes to the fence]

Smalls: I was gonna put the ball back.

Squints: But it was signed by Babe Ruth!

Smalls: Yeah, you keep telling me that! Who is she?

Ham Porter: WHAT?! WHAT?! [And then they just go off . . .]

Kenny: The sultan of swat!

Bertram: The king of crash!

Timmy: The colossus of clout!

Tommy: The colossus of clout!

All: BABE RUTH!

Ham Porter: [emphatically] THE GREAT BAMBINO!

Smalls: [in shock and horror] Oh, my! You mean that's the same guy?![16]

We can sense something similar happening with the apostle Paul in his letter to the Colossian church, where we find Christ's peacemaking work on full display in Colossians 1:20. This portion of the letter is one of the Christological highpoints in the

---

[16] *The Sandlot*, 1993. Exchange found online at https://www.quotes.net/mquote/126753. Accessed May 4, 2020.

New Testament. In hymnic language, the apostle Paul paints us a stunning portrait of Jesus Christ.

After mentioning Christ's redemption in Colossians 1:12–14, Paul erupts in praise to Christ. Notice how often "he" is directly referred to—Paul uses the word "he" four times, and "him" is mentioned seven times! Paul can't get over Jesus. He goes on and on about Christ's glory, Christ's creation, Christ's power, Christ's deity, Christ's church, and Christ's cross. We're like Smalls saying, "Oh my, you mean that's the same guy?!"

But there's more. Paul goes from "And He" to "And you" (1:21ff NKJV). This glorious Christ has come *for you*! Through the work of the cross, he has reconciled us to God, giving us peace with God, granting us new life, and new power to pursue godliness and harmony in our relationships.

While this little book is mainly about our peace with others, it's important to fix our eyes on the ultimate peacemaker, the Lord Jesus throughout our study, as he is the place we find the empowerment we need to make peace with others. You will not pursue Christ-centered conflict resolution if your heart is not captivated by Christ. If Christ doesn't reign supreme in your life, then your peacemaking efforts will fall short. We cannot make peace with others horizontally without rightly worshiping the Prince of Peace vertically.

Indeed, Ken Sande speaks of the connection between Christ's peacemaking work and ours saying, "In addition to giving you peace with God, Jesus' sacrifice on the cross opened the way for you to enjoy peace with other people (cf., Eph. 2:11–22). This peace, which is often referred to as 'unity' (Ps. 133:1) is not simply the absence of conflict and strife. Unity is the presence of genuine harmony, understanding, and goodwill between people."[17]

Captivated by the Supremacy of Christ

If a peacemaker is first and foremost captivated by Christ, how do we get our hearts to that place of captivation? Many times, we simply forget the majesty of Jesus and we find ourselves wondering, *What makes Jesus so enthralling, anyway?*

One thing that makes Christ so captivating is that he is *supreme.* Throughout the letter of Colossians, the inspired apostle makes the argument that "Christ is enough." Christ is *sufficient* for salvation and sanctification. And that's wonderful. But how can we bank on the fact that he's sufficient? What makes him able to deliver on that promise that "he's enough"? Colossians 1:15–23 tells us—it's the *supremacy* of Christ which assures us of the sufficiency of Christ.

There are several passages in the Bible about the nature and work of Christ that sound more like poetry or hymns than they do mere sentences, because "regular old language" is simply inadequate to convey his glory. Colossians 1:15–20 is one of those.

---

[17] Sande, *The Peacemaker*, 46.

Not only does Paul give us some reasons why Christ is supreme, he does so in style. His uncontainable song pours out in this crescendo-building way: "This thing you are looking for, Christ is this for us, but not only this, he is *also* this other thing for us, and not only that, he *also* has power over these other sorts of things that only *God* could have power over, and on top of that, he is *also* this thing over here you probably couldn't have imagined, and *wait, oh wait, he's even more than that in this interesting way too—can you believe it?! He is everything!"*

Paul begins by highlighting ***Christ's nature***, as he says Jesus "is the image of the invisible God" (Col. 1:15a). That is, Jesus perfectly reveals the nature of God (see 1:19, 2:9; 2 Cor. 4:6; John 14:8; Phil. 2:6–7). You want to know what God is like? Look at Jesus. We don't believe in just some God of our imagination, but the God of revelation—perfectly revealed in Jesus Christ. You want to know how to reflect God's glory in relationships—even the ones that cause you conflict? Look to Jesus and pattern your life after him. So, Christ is supreme because of his nature. We may run to plenty of things to satisfy our souls or deliver us from our woes, but none of those things are divine. Jesus is better because he's God.

Next, Paul magnifies ***Christ's dominion***. Paul calls Jesus "the firstborn over all creation" (1:15b). Given that the whole passage is supporting the preexistence of Christ, this phrase cannot mean that Jesus was created. Jesus "always was wasing," as some have quipped. Look at the next verse also: "For everything was created by him, in heaven and on earth, the visible and the invisible, whether thrones or dominions or rulers or authorities—all things have been created through him and for him" (Col. 1:16). Jesus wasn't created; he's the One doing the creating!

So what does "firstborn over all creation" mean, then? This word "firstborn" (*prototokos*) has two primary meanings: (1) having priority in regard to time (or simply put, going first) and (2) being supreme in rank. Both are true: when we think of the time line of history, the Son existed before creation, and he is also supreme over it. But the main idea here seems to be the latter: status and superiority.

Does "firstborn" ring a bell in your mind? Of course it does. It's been used before when God says of David, "I will make him the firstborn, the highest of the kings of the earth" (Ps. 89:27 ESV). Firstborn is a title of *supremacy*. It's about having the highest-ranking position in a given realm. Christ is supreme over creation. In verse 16, Paul explains that "everything" was created *by* Christ, *through* Christ, and *for* Christ. His majesty is seen in the prepositions: "by" "through" and "for." Paul is going into every nook and cranny of existence and saying *all of it* was created by him through him and for him! Said another way, the one doing the creating is Jesus, the power necessary to create in the first place comes through Jesus, and creation itself was made for Jesus' glory! Whether we are talking about who started it, how it was made, or what its purpose is, everything having to do with creation is all about Jesus. So, Christ is supreme because he has dominion over the earth.

Yet Paul doesn't stop there. He continues to build, as he tells us it's not just the world that Christ has the highest seat over! His majesty is expressed in his power over visible and invisible powers—things on earth *and* in heaven. These invisible powers in the heavenly realm are called "thrones or dominions or rulers or or authorities" (1:16). Based on chapter 2, these may refer to evil forces, or good heavenly hosts, or both (Col. 2:8, 15). But Paul doesn't get into detail about them. His point is simple: Christ is supreme because he is sovereign over them all!

Knowing who Christ is—his nature and also every realm he has the highest-ranking seat in—makes a practical difference in your life, in your emotions, and in your relationships. There are evil forces at work in the world, but this is our Christ! We flee to him; we trust in him; we serve though him; we enter the work of conflict resolution knowing that this Christ is with us!

Next, Paul helps us ponder ***Christ's control***. He says, "He is before all things, and by him all things hold together" (1:17). In the original Greek language, this sentence actually starts with the word "And," reminding us that there is always more to Christ! Paul again asserts Christ's supremacy saying, "he is before all things" meaning that he has precedence over all things in time and status. But then he adds on yet another miraculous aspect of Christ: he is the one who sustains all things: "by him all things hold together." Christ sustains the whole universe (see also Heb. 1:3). He didn't create the universe and then take up his high-ranking position over it somewhere far away, aloft and aloof, letting things run on their own and leaving the humans to figure out how to keep the planets spinning. No, he has an active part in powering and sustaining everything he created. This is good news! One scholar said, "He [Jesus] keeps the cosmos from becoming chaos."[18] If Jesus can sustain the cosmos, then he can sustain us in our conflicts.

People often suffer from anxiety because they want to control more than they want to rest in Christ, who is in complete control. Often the desire for control either instigates an unnecessary conflict in the first place, or makes a conflict worse. Recognizing and embracing Christ's sustaining power allows you to rest; it allows you to trust in Jesus. He sustains everything moment by moment, and he can sustain us and strengthen us in our trials and frustrations. I love the old Gadsby hymn:

> Immortal honors rest on Jesus' head;
> My God, my portion, and my living bread;
> In Him I live, upon Him cast my care;
> He saves from death, destruction, *and despair.*[19]

---

[18] H. C. G. Moule quoted in David Garland, *Colossians and Philemon*. The NIV Application Commentary (Grand Rapids: Zondervan, 1998), 89.
[19] William Gadsby, "Immortal Honors Rest on Jesus' Head." Lyrics online at https://hymnary.org/text/immortal_honors_rest_on_jesus_head. Accessed May 4, 2020.

The Christ who sustains the cosmos is able to sustain you in your relational chaos. We don't have a puny little Christ. No, our Christ is supreme and sufficient!

As we might guess at this point, Paul's not done! He has more song left to sing, as he now highlights **Christ's church**. He says: "He is also the head of the body, the church" (1:18a). To be "the Head" of the church is to be the Lord over it. Christ is the Leader, the Chief, the Sovereign over it. Christ guides and governs his church, the redeemed people of God.

The second part of verse 18 gives us the grounds or reasons why he is the head: "he is the beginning, the firstborn from the dead, so that he might come to have first place in everything" (1:18b). Christ is the origin and source of life of the church, the fount of its being. This word *firstborn* we said can mean precedence in regard to time, or supremacy in rank. Here it is the idea of *precedence* that seems to be in view: Christ is the first to rise from the dead in true resurrected life (never to die again). He is the first in sequence! More will follow! You can think of it like "trailblazer," "pioneer," or the "pathfinder." He resurrected first, and we will follow in turn, when the time comes. What is true for Christ will be true for his people. In short, Christ is supreme because he took on death and won (no one has ever done that), he is Head and Shepherd of those who believe this is true in the here and now (no one else can do this), *and* he will raise those very believers from the grave and give them eternal life in the future (no one else can do this either). Supreme, indeed.

Why is this Christological point important when we are in conflict with others? Because it reminds us that we are resurrection people; we have guidance available right now from our resurrected Shepherd, we have power available from him right now as well, *and* we have hope for the future. Often in conflict one feels powerless and hopeless. But when your tank is empty, remember the tomb is empty!

The Supreme Act of Peacemaking

Are you ready for the high point of Paul's crescendo? After restating the deity of Christ (Col. 1:19), Paul puts the spotlight on ***Christ's crucifixion***. You can feel the descent from the heights above to the lowest of lows. The preexistent, fully divine Son of God, who created and upholds all things, who enjoyed the highest positions available in the universe, intentionally plummeted downward into unimaginable shame and pain. Where the world strives to go from the pit to the palace, the Son of God did the reverse. And he did so in a specific way: he came to earth and died on a cross: "through him to reconcile everything to himself, whether things on earth or things in heaven, by making peace through his blood, shed on the cross" (Col. 1:20).

The cross is the main focus of verses 20–23, and shows us what reconciling work really looks like. You can't miss it: *Jesus' reconciling work happens through the work of the bloody cross.* Paul underlines Christ's *cosmic* reconciliation in verse 20, and Christ's *personal* reconciliation in verses 21–23. Regarding the former, God chose to create the world through Christ; and in the end, God will reconcile the world through Christ. Notice the scope of it—"all things"—the whole created order (see Rom. 8:20–23). With great style and poignancy, New Testament scholar David Garland puts it this way:

> The death of an obscure Jew on a seemingly God-forsaken hill in a backwater of the Roman Empire attracted no notice from the historians of the era, but it was the event that reconciles heaven and earth. The world may be corrupted, disordered, and ravaged by sin, but God still loves it; and God intends for it to fulfill its destiny in Christ. Sin has defaced Christ's work in creation, but he came to undo its consequences and to bring concord in a universe out of harmony with God. How did he make peace in a conflict-ridden world? Paul says, "by the blood of his cross."[20]

This is Paul's way of pointing to Christ's atoning sacrifice. Christ's atoning work resolves conflict on a cosmic level, as it reconciles a runaway world back to its Creator. But, as I'm sure you can anticipate by now, Paul's not done. The atoning work of the cross also resolves conflict on a personal level. He adds:

---

[20] Garland, *Colossians and Philemon*, 94.

> Once *you* were alienated and hostile in your
> minds expressed in your evil actions. But now
> he has reconciled you by his physical body
> through his death, to present you holy, fault-
> less, and blameless before him—if indeed you
> remain grounded and steadfast in the faith
> and are not shifted away from the hope of the
> gospel that you heard. This gospel has been
> proclaimed in all creation under heaven, and I,
> Paul, have become a servant of it. (Col. 1:21–23,
> my emphasis)

This Christ cares about *you*. Though you were in conflict
with God, Christian, he has reconciled *you* to the Father. He has
made *you* a new creation. Isn't that astonishing!? This cosmic
Christ who created all things and sustains all things; this Christ
who rose from the dead and is the head of the church, the one
who plummeted down into the most painful of circumstances,
has come for *you*.

Notice *the nature* on Christ's personal reconciliation:

- The Means: *He* has reconciled us (1:22)—
  we did not do the reconciling or even initiate it. It's not us reaching up, but Christ
  taking the initiative and coming down.
- The Effects: We are now holy and without
  blemish, free of accusation (1:22).

- The Extent of Its Impact: The good news is proclaimed throughout the world (1:23; 1:6).

Notice also the *past*, *present*, and *future* dimensions of Christ's reconciling work:

- Past: You were alienated from God relationally, hostile toward God in your thinking, with a life marked by evil deeds (1:21).
- Present: *Now* he has reconciled you to God, giving you peace with God (1:22).
- Future: Genuine faith is persevering faith, "If you continue in the faith . . ." (1:23).

With all the glory of Christ expressed in this passage, we might assume Paul will keep going. But notice where he ends: the blood of the cross. It is the supreme act of reconciliation, the greatest example of a conflict resolved. There's nothing that rivals it.

What should all this mean for us and our relationships—particularly the ones where conflict continues to plague us?

Put off Grave Clothes, Put on Grace Clothes

If you were to ask a random Christian if he wanted to resolve his conflicts in a Christ-centered way, he would likely say yes. Yet many Christians don't realize that the impulse to resolve a conflict in a Christ-centered way comes from the habits of cultivating a Christ-centered *life*. If you are walking in Christ's ways in all of life, you will naturally resolve conflicts in godly ways.

So what might this way of life look like? Colossians 3 is an important passage for understanding what it means to live a Christ-centered life. Paul speaks of believers' union with Christ (3:1–4), and then exhorts them to *put off* all that is inconsistent with their new life in Christ (3:5–11), made possible through the reconciling work of Christ. Paul also says to *put on* all that is consistent with their new life in Christ (3:12–17). So Paul is calling for a spiritual wardrobe change of sorts—throwing out the clothes that our old, dead selves used to walk around in, and putting on new clothes that look a lot like what our Savior walks in.

Put Off. This "vice list" contains attitudes and actions that must not be part of a Christian's life (Col. 3:5–9). Paul tells us to put away sins related to sexual sin and greed (3:5–7) and sins related to fleshly attitudes and speech in relationships (3:8–9).

Paul adds that since we are new and are "being renewed in knowledge according to the image of your Creator" (Col. 3:9–10), we should live in a way that is consistent with this reality. The phrase "image of your Creator" (3:10b) recalls Colossians 1:15, where Paul says that Christ is "the image of the invisible God." Christians are being renewed in the image of Christ, and Paul tells the Corinthians that this spiritual transformation takes place as we behold Christ's glory (2 Cor. 3:18). Beholding leads to becoming. To be like Jesus, right down to the way we handle conflict, we must gaze upon Jesus.

A practical implication for this new life is the *unity* of believers (3:11): "In Christ there is not Greek and Jew, circumcision and uncircumcision, barbarian, Scythian, slave and free; but Christ is all and in all" (Col. 3:11). This is a wonderful passage to consider in regard to conflicts involving race, ethnicity, and background. In Christ, racial barriers are broken down. Religious/ethnic barriers are broken down. Cultural barriers are broken down. Social barriers are broken down. The gospel transcends these barriers! This made a powerful impact on the pagan world! And it can and will today!

The Christological climax of this portion of the passage says, "Christ is all, and in all" (3:11). Because Christ lives in each person, Christ unites us together. Paul isn't saying that these distinct characteristics are gone (race, ethnicity, background, and culture); after all, God appointed them for us, and they have great worth and dignity! Paul is saying that *being in Christ brings harmony* in our relationships. And when unity exists amid this beautiful diversity, the glory of Christ is magnified. But to have this, our identity in Christ must be more important than other identities.

Put On. At this point, we've thrown out our old grave clothes, and good riddance, but now we are exposed to the elements! What are we supposed to walk around the world in? Thankfully, Paul tells us what putting on grace should look like.

Paul notes these Christlike traits that we should walk in: *compassion*, *kindness*, *humility*, *gentleness*, and *patience* (3:12). Christ is known for these virtues, and Christ-followers must pursue them.

The apostle adds that Christians are to *bear with one another and to forgive each other* (3:13). Forgiveness is to be extended and experienced "just as the Lord has forgiven you" (3:13). Christ has forgiven us *freely*, *fully*, and *gladly*. He gives us the power and the pattern for forgiveness. Scholar N. T. Wright says it well: "First, it is utterly inappropriate for one who knows the joy and release of being forgiven to refuse to share that blessing with another. Second, it is highly presumptuous to refuse to forgive one whom Christ himself has already forgiven."[21]

When it comes to resolving conflict, we need to return to passages like Colossians 3:13 (as well as Eph. 4:32, Matt. 18:21–35) in order to allow the forgiveness of Christ to drive and shape our forgiveness of others. Our Lord stands "ready to forgive" (Neh. 9:17b ESV). The psalmist exalts the Lord who "forgives all your iniquity" (103:3). Growing into the image of Christ means that we are quick to forgive, and that we become slow to anger, abounding in faithful love (Ps. 103:8). Christ has canceled our debt through this death on the cross (Col. 2:14), so his people should follow suit, being quick to forgive and shatter

---

[21] N. T. Wright, *Colossians and Philemon*. Tyndale New Testament Commentaries (Grand Rapids: Eerdmans, 1986), 142.

their grudges. The reconciling love of Jesus motivates and shapes our reconciliation with others.

This idea of "bearing with one another" (Col. 3:13) is important because dealing with people can be difficult, especially with those that you live closest to! Paul then mentions what might be called the "overcoat" saying, "Above all, put on love, which is the perfect bond of unity" (3:14). How would our relationships change if we put on these grace clothes? Let's put them on. They might feel big at first—after all, they are patterned after Christ—but as we walk in them day after day, we will grow up into them over time, and they will eventually fit us like a glove!

The Peace of Christ. From the peace that Christ has made between sinners and God (Col. 1:20–23), Paul urges Christians to now "Let the peace of Christ, to which you were also called in one body, rule your hearts" (3:15a). The word *rule* is important. It originally meant to act as an athletic umpire. What Paul is saying is this: Christ's peace must give the final decision in regard to Christian conflicts. Let peace rule your heart individually, and let this peace be the goal in all your dealings with others.

When this peace is experienced, it's a sign of the inbreaking of God's kingdom, for when it fully arrives, there will be total shalom—no more conflicts! So let peace dominate your relationships, and if it's not, *pursue* peace when relational harmony is being threatened. Let us stand in awe of Christ, the supreme peacemaker, and imitate him. Let us "be thankful" (Col. 3:15b) for the peace that Christ has given us through his reconciling love, and may genuine thankfulness cause us to put away anger, and to put on compassion, kindness, humility, gentleness, patience. May we forgive others as we have been forgiven by Christ.

CHAPTER 3

The Fruit of the Spirit Displayed in Relationships

I usually expound on Ephesians 5 at wedding ceremonies, but on one occasion I decided to briefly highlight Paul's passage on the fruit of the Spirit: "For the flesh desires what is against the Spirit, and the Spirit desires what is against the flesh; these are opposed to each other, so that you don't do what you want" (Gal. 5:17). Why did I include such a verse in a wedding ceremony? To remind the couple that the biggest conflict they would face in their marriage wouldn't be between the two of them, but between the flesh and the Spirit! If a Christian husband or wife walks in the flesh, not the Spirit, then there will be problems in the marriage. The same is true for all relationships.

In *When Sinners Say "I Do,"* Dave Harvey writes, "Marriage is not a romance novel. Marriage is the union of two people who arrive toting the luggage of life. And that luggage always contains sin."[22] This may be difficult to accept in a culture that wants to redefine sin, rename sin, or blame others for their sin, but as Christians, we must embrace it. And this doesn't just apply to marriage! This is true of any two people in any sort of relationship—friend to friend, parent to child, pastor to congregant, or otherwise. Each of us carries baggage into our relational spheres.

Often, we reduce the reasons for our problems in relationships to communication breakdowns, being from different backgrounds, or having different temperaments. While many things can contribute to problems in relationships (and shouldn't be overlooked), the biggest problem lies within. G. K. Chesterton once responded to a newspaper article that invited people to respond to the question, "What's wrong with the world?" His reply was simple: "I am."[23] We must keep this in mind as we think on relational conflict.

Our Need for the Spirit's Help

Yes, it's a hard truth to embrace: we all have a lot of problems, but our biggest problem is *us*. But there's good news if we

---

[22] Dave Harvey, *When Sinners Say "I Do"* (Wapwallopen, PA: Shepherd Press, 2007), 15.
[23] Ibid., 16.

will accept this truth. Pastor from yesteryear Thomas Watson once said, "Till sin be bitter, Christ will not be sweet."[24] Until we see the reality of sin, we will not treasure the grace of the Savior. But we may also add, "Till sin be bitter, *the Spirit's power will not be sought*." When we recognize the real problem, we will go to the right solution. The failure to admit our depravity keeps us from seeing our desperate need for the Spirit's help. But if we can admit our problem, and rely on the Spirit, then we can see fruit in our relationships. The more I depend on the Spirit, and bear the fruit of the Spirit, the better husband, friend, pastor, dad, and neighbor I will be.

Indeed, though conflict will find its way into all our lives at some point, walking by the Spirit in everyday life changes the person handling the conflict. Said another way, the first way God helps you manage conflict in your life is not to change the circumstances or the other person, but to change *you* from the inside out by the power of his Spirit. Conflicts only change as the people involved in them change.

We see this sort of thing frequently in the stories we love most. Take *Good Will Hunting*, for example. Will is a troubled young man, and though he's a genius who can solve almost any problem, he somehow can't figure out how to solve his own personal issues that stem from his difficult childhood. He

---

[24] Thomas Watson, *The Doctrine of Repentance* (Carlisle, PA: The Banner of Truth Trust, reprint 2002), 63.

brawls on the street. He attacks government officials. Conflict and dysfunction follow him everywhere he goes. After attacking a police officer, he is required by law to see a therapist, and after a slew of them give up on him, he's introduced to the one unexpected counselor whose loyalty and help changes him for the better. Through this counselor's help, Will realizes that he no longer has to protect himself from pain or fear or loss. By the end of the movie, we don't see needless conflicts rising around Will anymore. And that's not because the world became perfect overnight; it's because *Will* changed over time, through the advocacy and love and help of another. In many ways, that counselor's work in Will's life is similar to what the work of the Spirit is like in you and me. Many of our conflicts arise simply because we are troubled inside, and the Spirit, our Counselor and Advocate and Helper, comes alongside us and helps us change over time.

Maybe you hear people talk about the work of the Spirit, and you want to distance yourself because you think all that "Spirit stuff" is for super-Christians, or "charismatic types" or "mystics" who live in the desert. Let me encourage to not think this way. Recognize that immediately after this passage on the fruit of the Spirit, Paul goes directly to *relationships* in the body of Christ (Gal. 6:1–10). Don't think, "I'm just a mom." Or, "I'm just a teenager." Or, "I'm just a dad." If you're a Christian, then you have the Spirit's indwelling presence, and you also need the Spirit's help in order to display the Spirit's fruit in your relationships.

Prior to Galatians 5:16, Paul has been expounding the good news that those who have trusted Christ are free in Christ. We are free from the burden of trying to justify ourselves by works. We aren't bound to the religion of "do" but the good news of "done," for Jesus has paid it all. But the problem is many interpret this freedom in grace as a license to sin. Paul urges us not to think this way. He doesn't want us to add the law to the gospel, but he also doesn't want us to use our liberty as a license to sin (Gal. 5:13). It's not a freedom to sin, but a freedom *from* sin that we have. And the way we live now is by the Spirit's work in us; for the Spirit doesn't lead us to sin but into Christlikeness. Paul says we "began by the Spirit" and we should "finish by the Spirit" (Gal. 3:3 ESV); and we must "keep in step with the Spirit" (Gal. 5:25 NIV).

We should all grasp that the reason we sin is not because of someone else's folly and rebellion, but because of *our* giving into the flesh. The person who cuts me off in traffic isn't the reason I yell something inappropriate or give the driver half of a peace sign, but it's because I gave into my sinful flesh. This doesn't excuse others' actions (they need to be dealt with); it simply means we need to tend to the issue in our own hearts (Mark 7:20–22). I can't control the actions of people, but I am responsible for responding in a certain way, and that response for the Christian is to live by the Spirit's help.

Walk by the Spirit

The flesh and the Spirit have competing agendas. We are new creations if we are in Christ, yes, but the battle rages on until Christ returns.

But this shouldn't lead us to a defeatist mentality. Paul tells us in Romans that we aren't slaves of sin any longer (Rom. 6:6–7, 14, 18, 22). We have been united to Christ, and we have the power of walking in the newness of life (Rom. 6:1–5). We can have significant and observable victory over remaining sin, as we refuse to let it reign in us (Rom. 6:12). We who know God's saving grace in Christ have said good-bye to the world of sin. We're new. This does not mean that we're not capable of sinning anymore, but rather, that our relationship to sin has changed. We died to it (Rom. 6:2). We have a new heart, and therefore don't want to go back to that way of life. These gospel realities give us hope as we consider the present battle within (Gal. 5:16–26).

Paul tells the Galatian believers four important truths about walking by the Spirit:

- First, we walk by the Spirit **_continually_**. To "walk" by the Spirit (Gal. 5:16a) indicates the need to yield to the Spirit every day and everywhere. We must meditate on the Spirit-inspired Scriptures and follow the Spirit's guidance in our relationships.

- Second, we walk by the Spirit *to overcome the flesh*. When Paul says, "walk by the Spirit and *you will not carry out the desire of the flesh*" (Gal. 5:16b), he's stating a *promise*. Those who yield to the Spirit daily have the promise that they will *not* gratify the flesh. There's no neutral ground. We're living in one sphere or the other. You cannot be walking by the Spirt and be harsh with your spouse at the same time. You cannot be walking by the Spirit the same moment you burst out in anger at your roommate.

- Third, we walk by the Spirit *because the battle is so intense*. The inspired apostle says that the flesh is "against" the Spirit and vice versa, and that these two are "opposed to each other" (Gal. 5:17). The enemy wants us to have a *casual attitude toward sin*. Paul is telling us that the Christian life is a *war*. Therefore, to conquer the flesh, one must see the seriousness of this battle and resolve to walk by the Spirit. Without his help, we have no shot conquering the internal conflict within us, or the external conflicts we have with others.

- Fourth, we walk by the Spirit *to be free from the law*: "But if you are led by the Spirit, you are not under the law" (Gal. 5:18).

Paul connects life in the Spirit to liberation from the Mosaic era. Believers in the new covenant are enabled to obey God by the new way of the Spirit, and bear fruit for God (cf., Rom. 7:4–6). We have new life in Christ, and new power in this new covenant, to offer ourselves to God. God has given us everything we need to showcase his love and grace in our relationships.

The Vices of the Flesh (5:19–21)

How does one know if he or she is walking by the flesh or the Spirit? Paul tells us in Galatians 5:19–23. The first list includes *the works of the flesh*:

Now the works of the flesh are obvious: sexual immorality, moral impurity, promiscuity, idolatry, sorcery, hatreds, strife, jealousy, outbursts of anger, selfish ambitions, dissensions, factions, envy, drunkenness, carousing, and anything similar. I am warning you about these things—as I warned you before—that those who practice such things will not inherit the kingdom of God. (vv. 19–21)

Sexual Sin. Paul notes sexual sin first in his other vice lists (cf., Eph. 5:3; 1 Cor. 6:9; Col. 3:5). So does Jesus in Mark 7:20–22.

Sexual immorality is a general word for all forms of sexual sin. *Moral impurity* often denotes sexual sin also (cf., Rom. 1:24; 2 Cor. 12:21; 1 Thess. 4:7). *Promiscuity* is also a common word for sexual sin (cf., Mark 7:22; Rom. 13:13; 1 Pet. 4:3; 2 Pet. 2:2, 7, 18). The reason for many relational problems can be traced to this desire of the flesh.

We must not simply try to manage this craving, but to put it to death. Sexual sin *grieves* the Holy Spirit. It *affects many others*, not just the one sinning. It displays *self-centeredness*. It *dishonors* those made in the image of God. It *violates* God's pure plan for marriage. It's *totally opposite* of the fruit of the Spirit, like love, goodness, faithfulness, and self-control.

Idolatry. The sin of idolatry may be literal (including the worship of images or other false religious acts like *sorcery*) or it may be functional heart idolatry (where we worship anything other than God as ultimate in our lives). In either case it's twisted and it leads to other sins. Sin problems are worship problems. When I get below the sin that's affecting my relationship with someone, usually I find an idol that needs to be uprooted and destroyed. I find something that is demanding my time, attention, and interest. I find something that I'm trusting instead of God. I find something that promises joy and satisfaction but only leads to despair. As the psalmist said, "The sorrows of those who take another god for themselves will multiply" (Ps. 16:4). Often idolatry leads to the multiplication of relational sorrows. The question, "Who is my God?" directly impacts my relationship with others. If I answer that vertical question with anything other than the One True God, I can expect horizontal, relational conflicts all around me.

Relational Evils. Next we find eight sins that are often wrapped up in conflicts. These sins are present in minor conflicts and are intensified in major conflicts.

- *Hatred* refers to hostility with someone.
- *Strife* refers to a contentious temper
- *Jealousy* can be used positively in the Bible to describe even God himself; however, here, Paul has in mind the wrong kind of zeal. A jealous person wants what another person has. This emotion often leads to other sins like bitterness and violence (cf., Gen. 37:12–36).
- *Outbursts of anger* is a work of the flesh, not a personality trait, and it has no place in relationships.
- *Selfish ambition* refers to the work of doing something out of rivalry, having self-centered and impure motives.
- *Dissentions* refers to division in a relationship.
- *Factions* probably emphasizes the "party spirit" that creates division.
- *Envy* is similar to jealousy. The envious person is not happy with God's gifts, and cannot stand it when others flourish.

Uncontrolled Desires. In this final group of sins, Paul mentions *drunkenness* and *carousing* (cf., 1 Pet. 4:3; Rom. 13:13). The latter probably referred to the drunken orgies that took place at the festivals of pagan gods, and secondarily "to the general insobriety of pagan life."[25] Living like an uncontrolled pagan is obviously in contrast to a biblical vision of a Christian relationship. And we shouldn't have to point out the connection between drunkenness and unhealthy relationships. Drug and alcohol abuse have destroyed individuals, friendships, and families.

Paul then ends with a warning, "those who practice such things will not inherit the kingdom of God" (5:21b). Those who come to faith in Christ by grace alone are new people (cf., Gal. 6:15). While they will still deal with sin and temptation, the flesh will not dominate them. Our good works do not save us, but true salvation leads to fruitfulness and faithfulness.

Till sin be bitter, Christ will not be sweet; till sin be bitter, the Spirit will not be sought. I'm grateful for the honesty of the Bible, as it tells me the real reason behind my misbehavior—my flesh. And this truth leads me to the Savior, and drives me to dependence upon the Spirit to be a faithful friend, husband, dad, pastor, and neighbor. And the same is true for you and all the relational hats you wear.

---

[25] R. A. Cole, *Galatians: An Introduction and Commentary* (Downers Grove, IL: InterVarsity Press, 1989), 217.

The Virtues of the Spirit (5:22–23)

The list of vices is contrasted with a list of nine virtues, which if cultivated, would transform any relationship:

> But the fruit of the Spirit is love, joy, peace, patience, kindness, goodness, faithfulness, gentleness, and self-control. The law is not against such things. (Gal. 5:22–23)

Notice that Paul says "fruit" not "fruits." God grows his people in every way into Christlikeness. As we abide in Christ, all of "the fruits" of the Spirit get produced.

Additionally, the fruit of the Spirit as a whole is basically a *character sketch of Christ*. The Spirit is conforming us into the image of Jesus, the one who perfectly embodied these virtues.

As a parent, I would love to "staple on fruit" to my kids. But these virtues must grow organically from their union with Christ. We simply cannot create Christlikeness apart from the Spirit's work. We need new hearts. As a parent, keep commending Christ to your kids prayerfully.

Love, Joy, Peace. It makes sense for *love* to appear first based upon the emphasis in Galatians. Here we see where the power for love comes from: *the Spirit*. Further, some of the other virtues mentioned in this list are practical expressions of love itself (*patience, kindness, goodness, faithfulness, gentleness*). Spirit-led believers express their *love* to God, "who first loved us" (1 John 4:19) and express a sincere *love* for others (cf., John 3:11–18).

The Spirit also produces *joy* (cf., Rom. 14:17). Believers can have joy even in the midst of trials because the Spirit has given them new affections (cf., 2 Cor. 6:10; 1 Thess. 5:16). The Spirit produces a life of satisfying joy, while the flesh only leads to dissatisfaction.

The Spirit creates *peace* in the life of a Spirit-led believer. Believers have the peace of God made possible through the cross work of Jesus (Eph. 2:14–17). Peace rules the hearts of those who submit to Christ (cf., Col. 3:15). Spirit-led Christians will also take on the role of peacemaking in relationships (cf., Eph. 4:1–6), to the glory of "the God of peace" (Heb. 13:20; 1 Thess. 5:23). It's hard to be in conflict with incredibly loving, joyful, peaceful people. And when you are, you want to get out of it quick. May the Spirit make each of us this sort of person!

Patience, Kindness, Goodness. Patience involves the ability to put up with others when it's difficult. A patient person is a long-suffering person. Patience is an attribute of God, who is long-suffering with sinful people. We need the Spirit's power to deal with our own children or spouses or coworkers, people in traffic, and those "interruptions" during the day. (I even find myself growing impatient with my kids right now, as I write on the fruit of the Spirit!) We all need to remember how patient God is with us, and pray for the Spirit to work patience in us.

Kindness is also a characteristic of God, and the Spirit reproduces this trait in God's people. Kindness involves being generous and benevolent to others—including those who aren't loving in return. By his grace and kindness, God brought us repentance and faith in Christ (cf., Rom. 2:4; Eph. 2:7, 4:32; Col. 3:12; Titus 3:4). Kindness is one of the most undervalued relational qualities and leadership characteristics. When evaluating a leader today, this characteristic often gets little attention, but it should (2 Tim. 2:24).

Goodness is closely related to kindness (cf., Rom. 15:14; Eph. 5:9; 2 Thess. 1:11). It speaks to the idea of doing good deeds and being generous (cf., Gal. 6:10).

Faithfulness, Gentleness, Self-Control. The person known for *faithfulness* is the reliable and dependable person. The faithful person keeps his or her word and fulfills their promises. It takes the work of the Spirit to produce such steadfastness in life, ministry, and marriage.

Paul mentions *gentleness* in other lists as well (cf., Eph. 4:2; Col. 3:12; Titus 3:2). In the next chapter, Paul highlights the need to restore the wayward brother "gently" (Gal. 6:1 NIV). He urges Timothy to deal with his opponents gently (2 Tim. 2:25), in order that they may repent. Gentleness connotes a humble posture and a genuine consideration toward others. The gentle person is not a pushy person, but one who lovingly serves others. Jesus, the gentle Savior, invites the weary to come and rest in him (cf., Matt. 11:29).

Finally, Paul ends this list of Christlike qualities with *self-control*. In contrast to the works of the flesh, like drunkenness and orgies, those who walk by the Spirit live restrained lives. The Spirit enables believers to have mastery over their passions. In our flesh, we are out of control, but by the Spirit we live self-controlled lives.

How can one live a life like this? Paul says by the Spirit. It does not happen by the law. For he says, "against such things there is no law" (5:23b NIV). In other words, you cannot legislate these qualities. Like Will Hunting, simply being told we should "do better" won't work; we need a person to come alongside us and help us not just behave better on the outside, but *become a different person* on the inside. And that's exactly what the Spirit does—he makes us fruitful from the inside out. The law can never produce this kind of fruitfulness. Praise Jesus we have more than the law; we have a person who can guide us, help us, and change us.

Encouraging Reminders

One could read this passage and think that the Christian life is a tug of war, and that we will have few victories and minimal growth, but the passage goes in a more positive direction:

> Now those who belong to Christ Jesus have crucified the flesh with its passions and desires. If we live by the Spirit, let us also keep in step with the Spirit. (Gal. 5:24–25)

Recognize and remember, Christian, as one adopted by God the Father, the hope and power you have in your new identity.

Christian, you belong to Christ Jesus. Something radical and powerful has happened to us. We have crucified the flesh (5:24). When did this happen? Paul seems to be referring to our *conversion* (see Gal. 2:20). When a person trusts in Christ alone for salvation they're uniting themselves with Christ, and saying *no* to their life in Adam. This death to the flesh brings about a new creation, and a deliverance from the present evil age (Gal. 1:4). While believers still feel the temptation of sin, these fleshly passions no longer have to reign—falling into them isn't a "given" anymore. Something decisively has already happened at the cross. Christ has won the ultimate battle, and now we have to deal with this mop-up operation until Christ comes to deliver us completely from this body of death. While we must daily "mortify the flesh" through spiritual discipline, our ultimate hope is that we belong to Jesus.

Christian, you possess the Spirit. Not only has our identity changed at conversion, but we also now have power to live every day by the Spirit (5:25). Again, while the passage reminds us of the intensity of the battle, we should be encouraged.

We belong to Jesus. And we have the Holy Spirit whose job it is to change us over time. When we know these facts, it gives us enormous hope to face our daily battle. We have what we need for victory, and as we grow into the image of Christ through the power of the Spirit, our relationships (and conflicts therein) become healthier and God-honoring. Our conflicts change as we change, and thankfully for us, we have everything we need to change!

CHAPTER 4

Overcome Evil with Good

Gideon. Esther. Rocky. Rey. The 1985 Villanova Wildcats men's basketball team. The 2018 UMBC men's basketball team. Dottie Hinson. Frodo Baggins. Katniss Everdeen. All of these: underdogs. Who doesn't love a good underdog story?

I'll tell you the individuals (or teams) who were *supposed* to win these contests. (Just ask the 1985 Georgetown Men's Basketball team, or the 2018 Virginia Cavaliers Men's Basketball Team how much they love underdogs.)[26]

One of the reasons we enjoy underdog stories is the fact that the underdog has to overcome so many obstacles. It's all very

---

[26] I'm indebted to Kent Bass, our Pastor for Counseling and Member Care, for his help on this chapter.

inspirational in a movie or athletic event, but when you step back into your own life, overcoming your obstacles in conflict isn't thrilling, is it?

Like a good underdog story, however, there's no shortage of obstacles for us to deal with: *pride, fear, anger, worry, doubt, anxiety, envy, jealousy, selfishness, strife,* and *idolatry* to name a few. Not to mention a host of circumstantial obstacles turn up the heat on our conflicts, like a global pandemic, screaming kids, unmotivated teenagers, an overbearing boss, an overworked spouse, unemployment, fatigue, slow internet, traffic jams, the weather, an empty fridge, long lines at the grocery store, an empty bank account, bad umpires, and the list goes on. There's a lot to overcome.

At the end of Romans chapter 12, Paul summarizes one of the most important aspects of navigating conflict: "Do not be overcome by evil, but overcome evil with good" (Rom. 12:21 ESV). This is the obstacle we all have to overcome if we are going to please Jesus in our conflicts. We must overcome *evil* with *good*. Regardless of who we are, where we live, or the uniqueness of our circumstances, this is our goal.

Peter also urges scattered Christians to think along those same lines (1 Pet. 3:8–12). Quoting Psalm 34:14, he says: "let him turn away from evil and do what is good. Let him seek peace and pursue it" (1 Pet. 3:11).

Jesus saved us by overcoming evil with good. And for marriages to endure, husbands and wives must overcome evil with good. For friendships to endure, friends must overcome evil with good. For churches to grow up into Jesus, brothers and sisters in Christ must overcome evil with good.

In Romans 12:9–21 we gain invaluable insight on what this entails. Paul highlights several countercultural actions that should mark the Christian, but I want to highlight those that are more directly related to verse 21, "overcome evil with good" (ESV).

Detest Evil, Cling to What Is Good

Paul begins this passage saying, "Let love be without hypocrisy. Detest evil; cling to what is good" (Rom. 12:9). Love serves as a heading for this passage and the following verses expand on it in some way (I'll also take up this subject more in the next chapter).

It's easy to gloss over the command to "detest" or "abhor" evil and to "cling to what is good." But we need to underscore it, as we think about relationships. We are called to *detest* evil.

This leads to a lot of questions. Does sin disgust us? Is it revolting? Do we hate what is evil? Notice that there are *no* qualifiers. No, detest all evil.

This raises another question: Do we think our own sin is as *detestable* as the sin of *others*? In conflicts, it's easy to see the other person's sin as worse or more problematic than our own. Jesus calls this *hypocrisy,* which is ultimately rooted in pride (Matt. 7:1–5). If you think your sin is less detestable, less significant, or less problematic than the person you are engaged in conflict with, then you are showing how blinded by pride you really are. Overcoming evil with good means abhorring *our own* sinfulness in the midst of conflict. It means having a desire and willingness to deal with *our own* sin before we criticize or deal with the sin of others.

Far too often, we soften our sinfulness. We say we're "struggling" to be gentle. We say we have an anger "problem." We have an "issue" with our language. If we soften the reality of sin in our lives, chances are we won't take the appropriate steps to kill it in our hearts. Theologian Cornelius Plantinga, in his book *Not the Way It's Supposed to Be*, helps orient our understanding of evil and sin. He says,

> Let us say a sin is any act any thought, desire, emotion, word, or deed—or its particular absence, that displeases God and deserves blame. Let us add that the disposition to commit sins also displeases God and deserves blame, and let us therefore use the word sin to refer to such instances of both act and disposition. Sin is a culpable and personal affront to a personal God. . . . God hates sin not just because it violates his law but, more substantively, because it violates shalom, because it breaks the peace, because it interferes with the way things are supposed to be. (Indeed, that is why God has laws

against a good deal of sin.) God is for shalom and *therefore* against sin. In fact, we may safely describe evil as any spoiling of shalom, whether physically (e.g., by disease), morally, spiritually, or otherwise.[27]

We spoil peace all the time, every day. We spoil it with our words. We spoil it with our actions. We spoil it with our attitudes. Spoiling shalom is sinful. Spoiling shalom is evil. So how do we overcome this?

We overcome evil by setting our hearts and minds on Jesus. Our love for Jesus must be greater than our love for *self*. In his collection of devotionals entitled *The Inner Life*, medieval scholar Thomas à Kempis said, "If you seek Jesus in all things, you will surely find Jesus. And if you seek yourself, you will surely find yourself, but only to your ruin. For a man who does not seek Jesus does himself greater hurt than the whole world and all his enemies could ever do him."[28] How many ruins have we created by seeking our own interests in our conflicts instead of seeking Jesus?

One of the beauties of the gospel is that we can actually go one step farther than setting our mind *on* Jesus. We have the ability to think *like* him. You've heard Paul's famous words before,

---

[27] Cornelius Plantinga, Jr., *Not the Way It's Supposed to Be* (Grand Rapids: Eerdmans, 1995), 13–14.

[28] Thomas à Kempis, *The Inner Life* (New York: Penguin, 1952), 33.

no doubt: "Do nothing out of selfish ambition or conceit, but in humility consider others as more important than yourselves. Everyone should look out not only for his own interests, but also for the interests of others. Adopt the same attitude as that of Christ Jesus" (Phil. 2:3–5). In your Bible, you may notice the heading over Philippians 2 which says something along the lines of "Christ's Example of Humility." This is very true. Jesus is our great *example* of humility. But he is more than that to us. He is our *empowerment* for humility as well! Let this truth soak in, Christian: *You have the mind of Christ*. It has been given to you. Use it to lay down your pride in the midst of conflict.

The pastors at our church have witnessed couples hold onto and fight for their own interests more than they are willing to hold onto and fight for the interests of their spouse; more than they are willing to take up the humility of Jesus. An important question we often raise is: "What are you willing to let stand in the way of a healthy marriage?" No one is usually quick to answer this question, at least with their words. But time and time again, their actions speak loudly. Often times, neither party wants to "die" first, and so pride, selfishness, and self-interest continue to stoke the fire of sinful conflict. By the grace of God, let us detest these things and hold fast to Christ. Let's be willing to die first, just as our Savior was.

Bless Those Who Persecute You; Bless and Do Not Curse

This verse (Rom. 12:14) sounds upside down, doesn't it? Blessing someone who persecutes us—why would we do this?

This is another verse that is easy to read over quickly, especially for Christians because we have been trained in an insufficient manner. We know we are supposed to be *nice* to people, so we try not to yell at waiters when they're rude or inefficient. We know we aren't supposed to get back at people when they offend us. But the problem with simply being nice or not getting back at people is that it doesn't fulfill this command. We are called to *bless* those who persecute us. Why? Because this is the fruit of the gospel.

Jesus blessed the very ones who persecuted him. Not just the Romans. Not just the scribes. Not just the Pharisees. He blessed you and me. Not only did he bear the weight of our sin on the cross, but he has lavishly poured out his kindness on us. Jesus didn't hold back his grace, not even on the ones who sinned against him.

Blessing those who curse you takes God's enabling grace, for this is not our fallen instinct. It requires prayer, and a life offered up to God in sacrificial obedience to his glory (Rom. 12:1–2). It involves thinking with a renewed mind (Rom. 12:2).

To be clear, seeking to bless those who sin against us doesn't mean we don't address their sin. It is often times appropriate to show our brother or sister their sin. In fact, we have a responsibility to do so, as we have seen in Matthew 7. However, we must ask ourselves, "Do I have a stronger desire to point out the faults of others than I do to bless them?" Instead of pointing the finger of accusation, let's extend the hand of grace. Let's follow the path of our Savior as we bless those who sin against us.[29]

Do Not Repay Evil for Evil

Many sinful conflicts would be avoided if this verse was burned into our hearts: "Do not repay anyone evil for evil. Give careful thought to do what is honorable in everyone's eyes" (Rom. 12:17). The presence of sin is bad enough, but we make it worse by how we respond. Clearly, we are not overcoming evil with good when we are returning evil for evil.

Think about the great game of beach volleyball. This is one of my favorite things to do at the beach. I love it when the two teams get locked in a back-and-forth rally. The excitement and tension builds. That's fun in volleyball, but we shouldn't be doing this sort of thing in conflicts. We aren't to return evil for evil! Yet, when we operate in the flesh, we do just this: send sinful words and actions right back at our opponent. And sometimes

---

[29] This verse has unfortunately been used to justify abuse in the church, which brings shame to Christ's name, Christ's Word, and Christ's people. Please see the Appendix in the back of this book for a separate word on abuse.

the hateful words and action can be like a volleyball spike on the other person's face! Don't play verbal or physical or emotional volleyball with people. You will face the temptation to do so, but responding to sinfulness with sinfulness doesn't honor the Savior, it doesn't reflect the Savior, it harms the other person, and it doesn't help you. Jesus shows us the better way, which is the way of the cross.

Consider the life of Joseph as an Old Testament example. His brothers treated him with great evil. In jealousy and hatred, they sell him into slavery and lead his father Jacob to believe that Joseph was killed by a wild animal. Years later, the brothers had a front row seat to his rags-to-riches story. Joseph had gone from slave to trusted servant, then from prisoner to superintendent of the royal granaries, being second in rank to Pharaoh in Egypt. Eventually the long-lost brothers come to Egypt in search of food in the midst of a famine. They meet Joseph but don't recognize him. He recognizes them and questions them about the rest of the family. They are at Joseph's mercy. Joseph has the ability and the power to return their evil upon them and to lash out in anger for the way they treated him. But Joseph, as a foreshadowing of Jesus, chooses a better way. He lavishes his family with grace and mercy, demonstrating reconciling love, and even providing for their needs (Gen. 45)! Let's follow Joseph's model, who points us ahead to an even greater model, Jesus.

Do Not Avenge for Yourselves; Instead Leave Room for God's Wrath

Overcoming evil with good also looks like this: "Friends, do not avenge yourselves; instead, leave room for God's wrath, because it is written, Vengeance belongs to me; I will repay, says the Lord" (Rom. 12:19).

If you don't think you are susceptible to vengeance, you don't have a very accurate perception of yourself. I don't necessarily mean a Wyatt Earp, *Tombstone* type of vengeance ("You tell 'em I'm comin', and hell's comin' with me!"). You might not be out for literal blood in the way you respond to conflict, but that does not mean you aren't vengeful. Apart from God, you are. So am I.

Vengeance is not only about the *magnitude* of the act, but also about the *motivation* of the act. We all find ways to pay people back for the wrong they do to us. Sometimes it's aggressive and visible, like a child pushing his sister because she took a toy from him. Sometimes it's passive and disguised, like a husband giving his wife the silent treatment because she criticized his decision he recently made for the household. If you have ever mistreated someone who mistreated you, then you have sought out vengeance. The punishment for sin, however, belongs to God, not me or you. Because of sin, we are constantly faced with the temptation to wrestle control and power away from God.

In Romans 12:19, Paul is saying that God's promise "I will repay" should help overcome our feelings of bitterness, resentment, and revenge. John Piper comments on this verse saying, "The promise that frees us from an unforgiving, bitter, vengeful spirit is the promise that God will settle our accounts."[30] So let's trust God to do this.

This is what Jesus did. He trusted God in the midst of unjust suffering. Peter says that Jesus has left us an example to follow: "For you were called to this, because Christ also suffered for you, leaving you an example, that you should follow in his steps. He did not commit sin, and no deceit was found in his mouth; when he was insulted, he did not insult in return; when he suffered, he did not threaten but entrusted himself to the one who judges justly" (1 Pet. 2:21–23). Let us entrust our situation to our God who judges justly!

This doesn't mean we do nothing, for pursuing justice is important. God has ordained certain authorities to administer justice on earth (cf., Rom. 13:1–7). Biblical writers urge us to pursue justice in all our dealings (e.g., Mic. 6:8). And we should desire justice for everyone. But we don't pursue *revenge*, for God will execute divine wrath on the last day; therefore we can trust him and not avenge for ourselves.

Trusting God is vital to our efforts in navigating conflict in a Christ-centered way. Often times we don't believe that trusting him will produce a better outcome than taking matters into our

---

[30] John Piper, "Give God Your Revenge." Devotional available at https://www.desiringgod.org/articles/give-god-your-revenge. Accessed May 4, 2020.

own hands. Yet if we want to make peace in our relationships, we have to trust that God is a faithful judge and believe that obedience to him is better than choosing our own way.

We have a lot of obstacles to overcome if we want to please God in our conflicts. Evil always lies close at hand when the pressures of life intersect with our heart. Some of those obstacles are obvious: pride, jealousy, anger, selfishness, and vengeance. Some of those obstacles are less obvious: sarcasm, silence, isolation, avoidance, and passivity. If we are going to make peace, we must have a commitment to overcome the evil in our own hearts, as well as the evil we experience from others.

When it comes to our internal idols and relational conflicts, we are all underdogs. Apart from Christ, evil is the clear winner. It should win—that is, if we were facing it alone. But we aren't. We have Jesus, the ultimate overcomer. He is the greatest example of overcoming evil with good. He abhorred evil and held fast to good. He blessed those who persecuted him. He didn't repay evil for evil. He trusted God to punish sin and didn't take matters into his own hands. Abide in him. Trust the way of his cross. He knows the path of peace, and he invites us to walk it with him. May the gospel, in its upside-down pattern and its unbeatable power, be large in your heart as you live like Jesus in the midst of conflict.

CHAPTER 5

Love One Another

When I was in college, I had a computer class where I learned to do this thing called "email." I thought it was the dumbest thing ever. I said, "No one will ever use this." Obviously, I missed that prediction.

I appreciate technology as it provides me with the ability to listen to sermons and lectures, share my sermons via podcast, and send video lectures to students. It's nice to be able to text my parents, and to Zoom with friends . . . but technology will never be a substitute for *embodied relationships*. After about two weeks of Zoom meetings during COVID-19, I was tired of talking to all my "flat friends." (I was also tired of looking up some of their noses due to their inability to rightly position the camera!)

The letters of John speak of the value of embodied relationships. He writes: "Though I have many things to write to you, I don't want to use paper and ink. Instead, I hope to come to you and talk face to face so that our joy may be complete" (2 John 12). John says there are limits to pen and ink (or for us, emailing/texting/zooming). He longs for face-to-face interaction—in order to complete their joy. Emails, texts, virtual meetings are helpful, but they can never replace real presence. You can't give a hug over Skype; you can't receive a holy kiss on Zoom. Something is lacking when we can't access the physical company of others. John says something similar at the end of 3 John: "I have many things to write you, but I don't want to write to you with pen and ink. I hope to see you soon, and we will talk face to face" (3 John 13–14).

One reason why you enjoy embodied relationships and experiences better than virtual ones is because you are a holistic being—heart, soul/spirit, mind, and body. Your personality will come out to a degree in an email or social media post, but because you are a physical being, part of what you want to communicate will never come through quite right without body language. Also, you have feelings. You have imaginations. You have reactions. You have eyes, and as Tony Reinke so aptly reminds us, eye contact is one of the strongest forms of social connection possible.[31] You have the capacity to embrace a friend you haven't seen in a long time, or to weep with a church member who falls into

---

[31] Tony Reinke, *12 Ways Your Phone Is Changing You* (Wheaton, IL: Crossway, 2017), 60.

your arms after hearing tragic news. You aren't a "flat" being; you are a whole, three-dimensional, multi-layered, complicated being that needs to interact in real time and space. No amount of technology will change that.

One of the most radical things you can do today is have a face-to-face conversation with someone (without looking at your phone every five minutes). It's sad to hear of families who spend little time talking about life, dreams, fears, and joys. Kimberly (my wife) and I are far from perfect parents, but we have tried to prioritize meals around the table as a family.

The incarnation teaches us about embodiment. The Word became flesh and dwelt among us (John 1:14), or "moved into the neighborhood" as Eugene Peterson paraphrases it.

We are made for relationships. When someone is dying, they don't care about their trophies, degrees, or accomplishments. They want people around them. From where I sit now in the current Coronavirus pandemic, one of the most tragic aspects of the crisis are the stories of people dying *alone*. As the church undergoes a time of physical separation from one another, many are now coming to realize what the Bible has said all along: it's a privilege to have friends, family, and biblical community (cf., Eccles. 4:9–12).

So how can we experience joy in those relationships? John provides the answer in 1 John 3:11–18: with love toward one another.

> For this is the message you have heard from the beginning: We should love one another, unlike Cain, who was of the evil one and murdered his brother. And why did he murder him? Because his deeds were evil, and his brother's were righteous.
>
> Do not be surprised, brothers and sisters, if the world hates you. We know that we have passed from death to life because we love our brothers and sisters. The one who does not love remains in death. Everyone who hates his brother or sister is a murderer, and you know that no murderer has eternal life residing in him. This is how we have come to know love: He laid down his life for us. We should also lay down our lives for our brothers and sisters. If anyone has this world's goods and sees a fellow believer in need but withholds compassion from him—how does God's love reside in him? Little children, let us not love in word or speech, but in action and in truth. (1 John 3:11–18)

Whether you're interested in flourishing in marriage, in a friendship, with your roommates, with your neighbors, or with your church members, this is an important passage for understanding the nature of *Christian love* (which naturally influences Christian conflict). There's a Johnny Cash Album entitled *Love, God, and Murder*. That's summarizes a good bit of this passage.

How can we love and not murder; how can we reflect God's love to others? John points out six features of Christian love, which if obeyed, will make a massive difference in the way we handle conflict, and respond to it too.

Christian Love Should Characterize Christ's People

John speaks of a "message you have heard from the beginning" (1 John 3:11). What is this message? John is referring to what the readers had heard when they first heard the apostolic gospel and the command of Jesus to "love one another" (3:23).

While methods may change from time to time, and various crises appear in different seasons of life, the heart of Christianity is unchanging. It involves loving one another, as John continually underlines in his letters.

Clearly in John's mind is our Lord's teaching, most notably his teaching during the Last Supper and farewell discourse in the fourth gospel (John 13:34; 15:12, 17). Up to John 13, the themes of John's gospel are both love and light; but then the focus turns to the disciples and the theme is exclusively *love*.

John tells us that Jesus "loved his own who were in the world" and that he "loved them to the end" (John 13:1). Then we read of the famous scene of Jesus washing the disciples' feet, teaching them about his cleansing grace, and exemplifying love and humility for them, foreshadowing his greatest display of love and humility at the cross (John 13:2–17). Then Jesus says to the disciples, "I give you a new command: Love one another. Just as I have loved you, you are also to love one another. By this everyone will know that you are my disciples, if you love one another" (John 13:34–35). Jesus exemplifies this love and also empowers it. He says that by this love, the world will know that we belong to him.

This command is issued again in John 15, as Jesus says: "This is my command: Love one another as I have loved you" (15:12); and "This is what I command you: Love one another" (15:17). This is the only commandment that begins this way, "This is *my command*." There are hundreds of commands in the New Testament but this one is referred to by the Lord of glory as "my command."

So, let's take it seriously. Let's take it as seriously as the command, "Do not commit adultery" (Exod. 20:14). Let's not think that we can somehow perpetually break it, or that it's optional. Our conversation with others is one way of keeping this commandant. Deeds of love are another. Love for one another should mark Christ's people. This isn't optional.

Christian maturity isn't merely about knowing Christian doctrine or being up on the latest movement in the Christian subculture. Maturity is about how we live; it's about how we love; it's about how we treat people—including the people that we may be at odds with.

Christian Love Is Difficult Because of the Evil One

John reaches into the Old Testament when he says that we should not be like *Cain*, "who was of the evil one and murdered his brother" (1 John 3:12). He says that he murdered his brother because "his deeds were evil, and that his brother's were righteous" (3:12b).

John goes to the early chapters of Genesis to describe what we should avoid and pursue when it comes to love. He tells us why it's difficult. Evil is present because the Evil One is at work. The devil is a liar and a murderer (John 8:44). Do you ever take a moment to acknowledge this in your everyday conflicts? Do you ever consider that what you are really running into is the devil at work? What would change if you realized this was happening in the midst of your common disagreements or moments of strife?

From Cain, we learn what we must avoid: *jealousy* (1 John 3:12). Sin enters the world in Genesis 3, and the sin of jealousy leads one brother to kill another brother. Cain was jealous of his brother's righteousness. His brother's offering was accepted while his wasn't. His response involved hate. This hate turned to murder (cf., James 4:1–2).

In Christ, you have a new identity: you are your brother's keeper, not killer. Don't be like Cain. Cain is an example of a child of the Evil One, with no spiritual life. The fact that he overcame his conflict with evil proves this to be true, where a child of God would have resolved their conflict with good.

In this ancient account, this truth is proclaimed: "sin is crouching at the door" (Gen. 4:7). Because of this, we need the power of the Spirit for harmony to reign in our relationships with others. If you find yourself in a "killing" mentality instead of a "keeping" mentality—if you find yourself jealous and angry— beg the Spirit to help you be more like Christ, and to fight the Evil One, and he will help you!

Christian Love Attracts Some People but Angers Others

Isn't it interesting that John says that some people in the world will "hate us" (1 John 3:13) even when we are seeking to love others?

With the example of Cain and Abel, John points out a pattern that has existed throughout the ages. Some are attracted to Christians' virtue, including their love for one another (cf., Acts 2:42–47; John 13:34–35). Francis Schaeffer called love for one another "the Final Apologetic," because love often persuades some people to believe the gospel.[32] But others are repelled by it, and even grow hostile in reaction to it.

Jesus puts these two together: love for one another and hatred of the world (John 15:9–25). He says, "If they persecuted

---

[32] See Timothy George and John Woodbridge, *The Mark of Jesus* (Chicago: Moody, 2005), 19.

me, they will also persecute you" (John 15:20). Jesus was killed, like Abel was killed, though he was righteous. Even though we know the death of Jesus was for the salvation of sinners, it was still innocent blood that was shed. So we shouldn't be surprised if others hate us for loving like Jesus.

Some professions are inherently dangerous. Soldiers will get shot at occasionally. They shouldn't be surprised by it. Race car drivers shouldn't be dumbfounded when accidents happen on the track. Baseball players shouldn't consider it strange or bizarre if they get hit with the baseball. And Christians shouldn't be surprised when the world hates us. They hated Jesus too. It's part of what we sign up for when we come to him. But let's follow the way of Jesus anyway because it is the way of life.

Christian Love Is a Sign of Genuine Conversion

Maybe you've picked up this book and you're not a Christian. I'm glad that you're reading it. I became a follower of Jesus in college. The gospel changed my life in powerful ways, including in my relationships. Before conversion, I had a terrible temper (one that is not completely gone, I confess, and one that I must put to death daily), but after meeting Christ, he gave me a capacity to love that I didn't have before.

John says this is one of the signs that we have "passed from death to life" (1 John 3:14). We now love "our brothers and sisters." Love for others isn't the basis for conversion, but it's evidence of it. In contrast, John says that "the one who does not love remains in death" (3:14b). This idea surrounds these verses (see 3:10; 4:7–12). Faith and love are tied together in the New Testament (see Gal. 5:6).

To practice Christian love in our relationships in our homes, apartments, and churches, we need something more than Jesus' example. We need new life. We need new abilities. We need a new nature. We can't follow Jesus and avoid the example of Cain, apart from the new birth. Through the gospel, God brings the dead to life and changes us. His love makes us loving disciples: "We love because he first loved us" (1 John 4:19). Those who embrace Christ are given the indwelling Holy Spirit, who enables us to truly and unselfishly love God and others. As the Spirit transforms us, the command to love isn't viewed as a burden but as a delight, because we are now able to do it (1 John 5:3)!

John adds, "Everyone who hates his brother or sister is a murderer, and you know that no murderer has eternal life residing in him" (3:15). He is not necessarily denying the possibility of repentance and forgiveness for a murderer (Paul persecuted Christians, Jesus prayed for the forgiveness of his murderers); but rather, John is talking about a present and abiding state of malicious hate and spirit of murder in the heart of a person, which shows that they have no spiritual life. Do you have hate in your heart? Perhaps this is the real reason behind much of your conflict with others in life. A Christian is someone with a new heart and one who lives with this new commandment written on it.

Physically, we go from *life* to death, but the good news of the gospel is that we get to go from *death* to life! If you're not a Christian, what Jesus holds out to you is not religious rules to follow, but new life and a new capacity to love.

Christian Love Is Cross-Focused

The cross shows us what love is. Cain's self-focused hatred led to murder—to *taking* life. Jesus' selfless love led to sacrifice—to *giving* life. John writes, "This is how we have come to know love: He laid down his life for us. We should also lay down our lives for our brothers and sisters" (1 John 3:16).

Some think of love as tolerance or lust or sentimentalism, but John cuts through the fog with this verse. Do you want to "know" what love is? It's this: Jesus laid down his life for us, and we are to lay down our lives for others. Do you take life from others, or give it? Do you lay down your life for others, or demand they lay down their life for you?

The cross shows us that Christian love involves a passion that leads to action. Jesus didn't merely say he loved us; he demonstrated it (Rom. 5:8). Jesus' love wasn't mystical, vague, or theoretical; it manifested itself in action. This means that if we're not making sacrifices for others in practical action, then we're not loving in a distinctively Christlike way. Christians don't love others in theory.

The redeeming work of Jesus shapes and empowers Christian love. When Paul exhorts husbands to love their wives, he doesn't say, "Husbands love your wives . . . because you should" or even "because I said so." But he says, "as *Christ* loved the church and gave himself for her" (Eph. 5:25). This is the model, gentlemen. When Paul exhorts us to forgive, he doesn't merely say "Forgive, because it's the right thing to do," but he ties it to Christ's redemption, "And be kind and compassionate to one another, forgiving one another, just as God also forgave you in *Christ*" (Eph. 4:32, my emphasis). Then in the next breath, he adds, "Therefore, be imitators of God, as dearly loved children, and walk in love, as Christ also loved us and gave himself for us, a sacrificial and fragrant offering to God" (Eph. 5:1–2). Everything from marital love to forgiveness is to be expressed through cross-driven, cross-shaped actions. Jesus is the central model for every way we relate to others, whether we are in conflict or out of it.

And there's more: the cross empowers this love. Christ's death was an atoning death. This redeeming work has a transforming effect. Look at what it did to the disciples! Consider John, Peter, Paul, and others. These were not soft, sentimental guys. James and John wanted to torch the Samaritans! Peter cut a guy's ear off with a sword! Paul was violently persecuting Christians! But then they would go on to write about *love,* becoming some of Christianity's first poster children for how to love and minister well to others. How? Because Jesus changed them. And his grace is transforming people today! Jesus can take angry dads, melt them, and make them gentle. He can take rebellious teenagers and make them gracious disciples. He can take bitter wives and make them kind and tender. He can take a hostile coworker or roommate or friend, and make them peaceful, warm, and kind. This is what Jesus does to people—he changes them into all that God wants humans to be.

Christian Love Involves Practical Acts of Compassion

John gets really down-to-earth here: "If anyone has this world's goods and sees a fellow believer in need but withholds compassion from him—how does God's love reside in him? Little children, let us not love in word or speech, but in action and in truth" (1 John 3:17–18). The notion of love as "warm fuzzy feelings" is blown out of the water. John isn't promoting sentimentalism but *action*.

The scenario is straightforward. Someone has resources and notices a fellow believer in need. But this individual "withholds compassion" and does not help the needy person. John says this is not love, even if one has "word and speech." Real love results in "action and truth." And notice the striking question, "How does God's love reside in him?" (3:17). Answer: it doesn't.

At the end of the day, kind words about love aren't what helps the person out. Having some abstract definition about love isn't needed either. Talk is cheap, as we say. Faith works. Love acts.

Let's drill down on this principle. If a man says he loves his wife, but never spends any time with her, and spends all of his time working, pursuing hobbies, or scrolling through social media, then John would question such a statement. If a wife says she loves her husband but likewise spends all her time working, pursuing hobbies, or scrolling through social media, then John would say, "Don't kid yourself." The truth in this scenario is that the husband and the wife actually love their work, their hobbies, and their devices more than each other—their actions are a clear demonstration of this. In short, love is more than words. It involves action. And if your actions don't demonstrate what you say you love, you don't really love that thing.

Don't simply love the idea of "loving one another," but actually love real people in your life—*demonstrate, demonstrate, demonstrate.* Let this command control your heart as you pull in the driveway and prepare to enter your home; or as you prepare to enter your church building, or as you walk down your neighborhood street.

This foundational passage is clear and challenging. But it's also *hopeful* as it shows us that we have been given everything we need to live out this vision for Christian relationships. Jesus has given us the pattern and power to love people. So let me encourage you to take daily opportunities to serve people in your web of relationships as you express your love to them. As you do this, you'd be surprised how much conflict is preemptively averted simply because people believe you love them, and are less likely to accuse you otherwise. And what's more, even if a conflict is necessary—and many conflicts are—resolving it will typically go smoother if you've demonstrated your love over time to the other person. Trust and credibility have been built, and the love proven between the two parties will be able to handle a multitude of sins.

Most of us will *not* die as martyrs. Some will. And we should rightly admire them. But most of us will give our lives away, little by little, over the long haul, doing small things for our friends, neighbors, families, and church members. As one preacher said, instead of cashing everything in, in a blaze of glorious martyrdom, most of us will go around giving twenty-five cents away at a time, by doing things—simple things—that honor Jesus over the long haul. Deeds like visiting the lonely, taking groceries to the elderly widow, listening to our spouse who's having a difficult time, washing the dishes, forgiving the person who has offended us, planning a fun holiday for the family, surprising our roommate with an act of kindness, adopting an orphan, welcoming a foster kid, visiting a prisoner, or baking a cake for our neighbor—all of it done in the name of Jesus for the glory of Jesus. This is love.

CHAPTER 6

How to Be a Peacemaker

Over a decade ago, I preached a sermon series through the life of Christ, tracing our Lord's life chronologically through the four Gospels. What I remember most from that series is how many counseling sessions I had as we worked through various passages in the Sermon on the Mount. People confessed anger, lust, anxiety, marital conflicts, and more. I now tell aspiring ministers, if you preach through the Sermon on the Mount, prepare to do a lot of counseling!

But I didn't take this experience to be a burden; rather, I saw it as a blessing. When sin is exposed and dealt with, that's a sign of God's work in people's lives.

Jesus' famous beatitude, "Blessed are the peacemakers," is fleshed out in more detail in the Sermon on the Mount (and in later passages in the Gospels), and the rest of the New Testament builds on it. Further, there are many Old Testament passages that are echoed and deepened by Christ and the New Testament writers. What I would like to do in this chapter is identify "5 M's" for being a peacemaker, rather than a "peace-breaker" or "peace-faker."[33] How can we glorify God by pursuing peace, harmony, and unity with others? Here are five practical questions:

- **Me-First**—Is there a log in my eye?
- **Minor**—Can I overlook this offense?
- **Major**—Does this offense require the process of restoration?
- **Material**—Does this offense require restitution related to property, money, or other rights?
- **Mediation**—Does this offense call for another party to assist in peacemaking?

Me-First—Is There a Log in My Eye?

We touched on this idea before now, but we'd be amiss not to take a deeper look. Before we go point out the offense of another, we must first examine our own hearts. When we have a conflict with someone, the tendency is to point out all that is wrong with the other person, while avoiding our own sin. Jesus said:

---

[33] Sande, *The Peacemaker*, 22.

> "Do not judge, so that you won't be judged. For you will be judged by the same standard with which you judge others, and you will be measured by the same measure you use. Why do you look at the splinter in your brother's eye but don't notice the beam of wood in your own eye? Or how can you say to your brother, 'Let me take the splinter out of your eye,' and look, there's a beam of wood in your own eye? Hypocrite! First take the beam of wood out of your eye, and then you will see clearly to take the splinter out of your brother's eye." (Matt. 7:1–5)

Jesus had been talking about *hypocrisy* earlier in Matthew 6 and he returns to it here (7:5). This passage is about hypocritical judgment.

Again, Jesus does not mean that no one is qualified to comment on whether or not something is right or wrong according to Scripture. And he does not mean we shouldn't observe one another's lives for the sake of holding each other accountable or identifying false followers (in fact, he tells us to do that very thing later in verses 15–20, and Paul tells us to assess the lives of others inside the church in 1 Cor. 5:12 with the goal of purity and restoration). So *assessment* of another believer's life or actions is not wrong. There is room for making the right sort of "judgment calls" as we observe the lives of others.

Here in Matthew 7, however, Jesus is opposed to *hypocritical* judgment that fails to consider one's own sin first; he's opposed to a judgmental attitude that fails to consider the "log" in one's eye. The big problem here is that we cannot *see* correctly until we remove the log (v. 5). Our assessment of the other person is wrong; in other words, because something is blurring or blocking our vision. And it's not a speck—it's a 2 x 4! Jesus is saying our vision and observations about others in the midst of conflict is *totally* compromised when we fail to assess ourselves first. Pride compromises our ability to see anything accurately; everything is out of proportion, fuzzy, foggy, and wrong. Once the pride is removed, and the foggy goggles come off, we will be able to *accurately* assess the other person's life and actions. Once we do, we will likely consider their offense as a harmless speck compared to our log, and have the right heart in helping them remove it, free from anger or bitterness or resentment.

In the end, Jesus is helping us see the offenses on each side in proper proportion. While we most often think the other person has the log and we have the speck ("Sure, I can own up to about 10 percent of this conflict, but *they* are most certainly creating 90 percent of it!), Jesus flips this assumption around by telling us that most of the time, *we* are the major contributor to the problem! Professor Quarles states:

> Jesus then used this humorous illustration to demonstrate that disciples cannot aid their brothers in addressing their smaller sins until

> they first deal with their own more grievous
> sins. . . . The "hypocrite" is . . . consumed with
> pride and self-deception. He is blind to his own
> sin but keenly aware of the faults of others. He is
> devoted to *inspection without introspection*, care-
> ful examination of others without any sincere
> evaluation of himself.[34]

In a conflict, before I inspect others, I need to do some introspection on myself. Only until I do this, can I assist others in removing the speck from their eye.

I need to stop and ask myself some hard questions like: Do I have feelings of superiority? Am I bitter? Am I resentful? Have I murdered this person in my heart? Have I made unfair assessments about the other person's motives? Do I lack love? Do I want to inflict pain on this person? Why am I so angry? What am I trying to preserve? What am I trying to get? Am I considering how much I have been forgiven? It's very likely that some of these things (and more) are in my heart when I'm having a conflict with someone.

If there's sin in my heart, then I need to take it as a time to confess sin and repent. A good question to help aid confession and repentance is "In what ways am I creating 90 percent of the problem here?" Again, this is a gift of grace. Conflict often exposes sin and leads us to deeper godliness. It provides

---

[34] Quarles, *Sermon on the Mount*, 287–88, my emphasis.

us with an opportunity to uproot idols in our hearts, experience the freedom of grace, and return to the great commandment of loving God and neighbor. And it also helps us finally see others accurately as we engage with them!

Ken Sande points out that if we will deal with our hearts and confess our own sin and failure in a dispute, the other person will often respond similarly. He calls this "The Golden Result" saying:

> The Golden Result says that people will usually treat us as we treat them. If we blame others for the problem, they will usually blame in return. But if we say, "I was wrong," it is amazing how often the response will be, "It was my fault too."
>
> I have seen this result in hundreds of cases over the past twenty-one years. Whether the dispute involves a personal quarrel, divorce, lawsuit, or church division, people generally treat one another as they are being treated. When one person attacks and accuses, so does the other. And when God moves one person to start getting the log out of his or her own eye, it is rare that the other side fails to do the same.
>
> The Golden Result occurs most often with people who understand and cherish the gospel. When we admit that our own sins are so serious that Jesus had to die for us, and remember that he has forgiven us for all our wrongs, we can let

go of our illusion of self-righteousness and freely
admit our failures.[35]

It took me a while to realize that one of the keys to being
a good pastor is saying "I'm sorry" a lot. As a pastor, blindness
to your own sin is particularly acute—the goggles are especially
foggy for us sometimes—but after a number of conflicts, I realized that I often carry blame and must apologize and repent.
The same is true in a family. Saying "I'm sorry" a lot can change
the culture of your home. And I don't mean saying it mindlessly
or deceptively, but earnestly after a period of gospel reflection.[36]
And my confession and repentance will be more likely to elicit a
positive response from the other person.

Minor—Can I Overlook This Offense?

Some matters need to be overlooked. Author and researcher
Thom Rainer posted some of the silly things that churches often
fight over. Here are some of them:

- Argument over the appropriate length of
  the worship pastor's beard.

---

[35] Sande, *The Peacemaker*, 78.

[36] For an excellent article on this, see Alfred J. Poirier, "The Cross and
Criticism." Article available at https://www.thegospelcoalition.org/article/
cross-criticism/. Accessed April 28, 2020.

- A church argument and vote to decide if a clock in the worship center should be removed.
- A fight over which picture of Jesus to put in the foyer.
- A dispute over whether the worship leader should have his shoes on during the service.
- Two different churches reported fights over the type of coffee served.
- Major conflict when the youth borrowed a Crock-Pot that had not been used for years.
- An argument on whether the church should allow deviled eggs at the church meal.
- Some church members left the church because one church member hid the vacuum cleaner from them.

Rainer rightly concludes: "These issues are silly; many are absurd. They are really great distractions from the Great Commission."[37]

How much better would it be if we lived out this Proverb: "A person's insight gives him patience, and *his virtue is to overlook an offense*" (Prov. 19:11, my emphasis)? This underscores the New Testament idea of "bearing with one another" (Col. 3:13; Eph. 4:2). So many of our conflicts could be solved if we mercifully

---

[37] Thom S. Rainer, "Twenty Five Silly Things Church Members Fight Over." Article available at https://thomrainer.com/2015/11/twenty-five-silly-things-church-members-fight-over/. Accessed April 28, 2020.

overlooked minor offenses. Peter, alluding to Proverbs 12, tells Christians: "Above all, maintain constant love for one another, since love covers a multitude of sins" (1 Pet. 4:8; cf., James 5:20). When we love as we have been loved, we can overlook offenses.

When should we overlook an offense? This requires discernment, but some questions to consider would be the following:

> Was this act done unintentionally?
>
> Is this act an isolated incident and not a reoccurring incident?
>
> Was this act insignificant?
>
> Did this act harm others or the offender?
>
> Did this act harm the witness of the church?
>
> Is this act a non-moral one or a moral one? (Said another way, is this action due to simple differences in personality or preference, or is it due to overt sin?)

If we deem an act "minor," then Sande notes that to overlook an offense is *active*, not passive, because it requires you to mercifully *not talk about it, not dwell on it, nor allow it to grow into bitterness.*[38]

Overlooking a minor offense again goes back to the gospel, reflecting on the way God has treated us. Jesus told us to "Be

---

[38] Sande, *The Peacemaker*, 83.

merciful, just as your Father also is merciful" (Luke 6:36; cf., Matt. 5:7; James 2:12–13; Matt. 18:21–35). Let us "imitate God" as his beloved children (Eph. 5:1).

Major—Does This Offense Require the Process of Restoration?

A major offense is any offense in which a person's action *dishonors God, damages your relationship, hurts others, hurts the offender, or disrupts unity.*[39] These actions call for a restoration process.

At Imago Dei Church, we often talk about the need to have "awkward conversations." This category of "major" offense would call for such direct and often uncomfortable conversations.

Some call this "confrontation" but we should remember that if there's been a major offense, the goal is not to confront or rebuke (though we may need to do that), but to *restore*. The desire isn't about being proven "right," but about seeing healing and wholeness. This means that when we need to have an awkward conversation, our attitude should be one filled with grace and love (not one of harshness and anger) because the goal is to see restoration and renewal.

In Matthew 18, Jesus gave us a restoration process to follow. He said, "If your brother sins against you, go and rebuke

---

[39] Ibid., 151.

him in private. If he listens to you, you have won your brother" (Matt. 18:15). So "step one" in the process of conflict resolution is just between the two of you. The goal is to win your brother or sister and see them restored. And remember, before going to the offender, we need to deal with our own hearts and seek to be merciful and forgiving (Matt. 18:21–35). Jesus goes on to say that sometimes one-one-one conversations do not lead to restoration. If "step one" doesn't resolve things, a second step is necessary, where two or three others are brought in to help mediate the conflict. And then if no change happens, Jesus provides "step three": the matter is brought before the church (Matt. 18:15–20).[40]

Regarding step one, ("go to him/her in private") Galatians 6 serves as another important passage for understanding the nature of this process. Paul says, "Brothers and sisters, if someone is overtaken in any wrongdoing, you who are spiritual, restore such a person with a gentle spirit, watching out for yourselves so that you also won't be tempted" (Gal. 6:1). Notice the familial language used ("Brothers and sisters"). This implies warmth and love. Notice also what Paul says about the *restorer*. He says the restorer is "spiritual." Every believer has the Holy Spirit and could be called "spiritual," but I think Paul is picking up the flow of his previous section on the fruit of the Spirit (Gal. 5:22–26). If so, then "spiritual" simply means that the restorer is displaying

---

[40] For a helpful book on church discipline, see Jeremy Kimble, *40 Questions about Church Membership and Discipline* (Grand Rapids: Kregel, 2017).

the Spirit's fruit. This interpretation is supported by the other qualification for a restorer listed in Galatians 6:1, namely, the restorer must have a "gentle spirit." Finally, the restorer should be *careful*, watching out that he or she is not also "tempted" (6:1b). We must always be aware that we are not immune to falling ourselves. Be careful that you do not exalt yourself over your brother or sister. And be careful that you do not step in the same trap as you attempt to restore the person.

What I have found in these "awkward conversations" is that the Lord often shows up! Though you may begin the meeting somewhat nervously or anxiously, once you begin to deal with the matter, you sense God's presence at work in the midst of the meeting. It's almost as if God likes it when we seek reconciliation and restoration! Imagine that. So let this encourage you. You aren't alone when you have to have such conversations. Jesus has commanded you to do it, and more than that, he shows up when you obey it, empowering the whole thing! Christ is with you in conflict.

What about when someone has something against you— even if you feel like it's unwarranted? Even if they refuse to come to you with their grievance? This too necessitates a direct conversation for the sake of restoration, harmony, unity, and for the sake of our witness. Jesus said, "So if you are offering your gift on the altar, and there you remember that your brother or sister has something against you, leave your gift there in front of the altar. First go and be reconciled with your brother or sister, and then come and offer your gift" (Matt. 5:23–24).

Jesus commands us to initiate reconciliation. He doesn't tell us to wait for the other person to initiate (even if they should). Doing this will give you peace of mind. It will also build up the other person, protecting him/her from bitterness, anger, resentment, and unforgiveness.[41]

Notice I said that Jesus commands us to initiate *reconciliation*. You are not initiating conflict with the other person when you confront them; the conflict is already there. You are initiating the *resolution* of the conflict. You are initiating *peace*. And that is very Christlike! Though we create conflicts with Jesus often (and usually avoid him when we do!), he always takes the initiative to come to us and resolve things. Jesus is a peacemaker—he comes to us instead of waiting for us to come to him. He *pursues* peace with us, even when we are avoiding him. And when we initiate to others, we are being like him.

---

[41] Sande, *The Peacemaker*, 148–49. See Sande on special considerations like going to a nonbeliever, going to a person in authority, and dealing with abuse.

Material—Does This Offense Require Restitution Related to Property, Money, or Other Rights?

Sometimes the conflict extends beyond personal relationships into material issues. So certain actions will need to be included in the restoration process.

For instance, if your neighbor's tree falls on your fence because he failed to trim it properly, then you will need to deal with more than your feelings toward the neighbor. You will need to negotiate the next steps for repairing your fence. If your neighbor is to blame, you will want to be gentle and reasonable. Don't seek to take advantage of the situation, but rather "love your neighbor as yourself" (Matt. 22:39). If it had been your tree and your fault, then you wouldn't want a harsh, demanding neighbor trying to take advantage of you. Jesus said, "Whatever you want others to do for you, do also the same for them" (Matt. 7:12). You might be able to overlook the offense all together; but if it's a more serious issue, seek to be *gentle* (communicating graciously and respectfully, seeking to understand the situation, and considering the interest of others), and *reasonable* (identifying the problems, considering all the options, and coming to a like-minded agreement).[42]

If you're the one to blame for a matter in which you need to restore someone's money or property, I would encourage you

---

[42] Ibid., 228–45.

to remember Zacchaeus, a little man who experienced a big change. Jesus declared that salvation had come to Zacchaeus's house (Luke 19:9), and one of the evidences of this grace was Zacchaeus's statement, "Look, I'll give half of my possessions to the poor, Lord. And if I have extorted anything from anyone, I'll pay back four times as much" (Luke 19:8). Zacchaeus was ready to do more than apologize; he was ready to pay people back *four times* the amount he had extracted from them! This kind of spirit and action can pour out of us when we recognize the grace that Jesus has poured out on us.

Mediation—Does This Offense Require Another Party to Assist in Peacemaking?

I will limit this category to one biblical example found in Philippians 4:2–3. I call the whole passage in Philippians 4:2–9 "stuff Christians deal with." Paul addresses issues like *joylessness, lack of gentleness, anxiety,* and *impure thoughts.* But the first issue he raises is regarding a *dispute* between two Christians: "I urge Euodia and I urge Syntyche to agree in the Lord. Yes, I also ask you, true partner, to help these women who have contended for the gospel at my side, along with Clement and the rest of my coworkers whose names are in the book of life" (Phil. 4:2–3).

Not much is known about these women or the cause of their strife. They do seem to have an influential role in the church, for Paul mentions how they labored with him in gospel work (4:3).

The issue doesn't seem to be a doctrinal, but relational. While we don't know the exact cause of the problem, we can note the process for solving the problem.

First, Paul instructs the women themselves to resolve the matter by having the same mind ("to agree in the Lord," 4:2). This echoes Paul's previous teaching on unity and humility (Phil. 2:1–11).

After his plea, however, Paul calls for *assisted peacemaking* (4:3). Paul alerts the whole church to the problem and urges one called a "true partner" to "help these women" (4:3). In asking for help, Paul shows us the importance of others assisting in the reconciliation process.

In a conflict, you may need to get help. You may need a pastor, a counselor, or a trusted friend. Such cases aren't new; we find one right here in Philippians 4, in one of the best churches in the New Testament!

Finally, Paul reminds everyone why these two sisters should be reconciled: the gospel (4:3b). He states that their "names are in the book of life" (4:3; cf., Luke 10:20; Heb. 12:23). The common faith and a common hope of two believers should motivate and shape the restoration process.

So let me ask you, will you ask for help when needed to resolve a conflict? Are you willing to call upon a "true partner"— a small group leader, a wise Christian friend, a pastor, or oth- erwise—to help you when necessary? Or on the flip side, if called upon, are you prepared to give help by offering biblical instruction and genuine care? Are you prepared to play an important role of peacemaker?

Let's avoid the wrong responses in conflict: escaping or fighting. Let's deal with things rightly in a way that honors God by considering our own hearts first, by asking if this offense can be overlooked, by seeking to carry out the biblical reconciliation process, by restoring property if necessary, or by seeking someone's help to mediate the conflict.

Conclusion

The hope of heaven should inspire love on earth. I have always been struck by Paul's thanksgiving for the Colossians:

> We always thank God, the Father of our Lord Jesus Christ, when we pray for you, for we have heard of your faith in Christ Jesus and of the love you have for all the saints because of the hope reserved for you in heaven. You have already heard about this hope in the word of truth, the gospel that has come to you. (Col. 1:3–6a)

Paul highlights three particular traits in the Colossian believers, for which he gives thanks to God: (1) faith, (2) love, and (3) hope. It's interesting that Paul doesn't mention certain things about the church that get people's attention today (the church building, the style of music, etc.). Instead, the apostle puts his finger on the *traits* of the family of God: faith, love, and hope.

Wherever you see these traits, you should give God thanks. This holy triad is mentioned elsewhere (1 Cor. 13:13; 1 Thess. 1:3; 5:8). But here in Colossians, faith and love arise out of "hope" ("the faith and love that spring from the hope," 1:5 NIV). The gospel promises a certain hope and this hope transforms us. It produces in us a "love . . . for all the saints" (1:4).

Hope doesn't mean wishful thinking. Hope is a settled confidence about future glory (cf., 1 Pet. 1:3–9). Hope does a number of things for the Christian, like help us endure trials (cf., Rom. 8:18ff). But here Paul teaches us that the hope of heaven also inspires love. Notice this word "because" (Col. 1:5). Faith and love spring from the hope of heaven. Being truly heavenly minded leads to love. How can you love people when they've been unloving to you? Dwell much on the hope of the gospel.

This is very relevant when dealing with a conflict. Ask yourself, "Am I thinking too earthly?" Setting your hope on heaven puts our differences with others in their proper perspective. Some issues are downright petty in view of eternity; so we should squash them. Many of the rivalries that exist between Christians, churches, and institutions don't display heavenly minded attitudes; they are selfish and earthly. In major conflicts we must also keep coming glory in view so that we can rightly restore and love people on Earth.

Jonathan Edwards called heaven "a world of love."[43] The hope of heaven inspires us to love others now, and it also reminds us that *one day there will be no more conflict.*

In this little book I have sought to draw our attention to the Lord of heaven, Jesus Christ, and to apply key biblical texts on this matter. May we press on in faithfulness and love. Let's pursue peace together; let's follow the pattern of Jesus in the power of the Spirit; let's display the fruit of the Spirit in our relationships; let's overcome evil with good; and let's love one another as Christ has loved us. Let's fix our gaze on heaven together, and seek to be like our Great Peacemaker who sits there, at the right hand of God, even now.

For soon we shall see that Prince of Peace, and he will wipe away every tear from our eyes, and usher in total peace forever and ever.

Maranatha . . . Come, Lord Jesus.

---

[43] See Dane C. Ortlund, *Edwards on the Christian Life* (Wheaton: Crossway, 2014), 167–75.

A Word on Abuse

Romans 12:14 and many verses like it, have been used to cover up abuse in various churches in our nation (and around the world); protect those who have harmed Christ's sheep in deplorable ways; and coerce abused church members to keep silent instead of reporting to their local civil authorities and trusted church leaders. We must reject this erroneous reading of the text, and this awful application of it.

Romans 12 is followed by Romans 13, which affirms the good and protective nature of government, telling us to submit to its authority. Part of obeying the law of our land is reporting abuse. I encourage any pastor, church leader, or church member who hears an account of abuse to report it not only to their church leaders, but the civil authorities, following any and all regulations that their local or federal government requires.

Also, if your church isn't informed on abuse or how to handle it, I recommend *Becoming a Church that Cares Well for the Abused*—a training curriculum for your church leaders to go through together. Please head to ChurchCares.com to obtain the curriculum and accompanying videos, where leaders and experts from all sides of the conversation—pastors, counselors, law enforcement officers, lawyers, social workers, and so on—equip you to handle abuse in your church the right way.

At our local church, the elders have tried to create a culture that cares well for the abused. We have made several statements in public worship, like this one:

> Abuse in any form is evil and must not be tolerated.

> This applies to situations not limited to male abuse of women. However, the majority of cases of abuse involve men abusing women (emotionally, verbally, physically, sexually . . .).

> A husband in particular is called to sacrificially love his bride, as Christ loved the church, therefore, abuse defaces this depiction of Christ's love for his bride.

> The elders of Imago Dei are ready and willing to protect the abused and call the abusers to full account and repentance—both legally and spiritually.

Churches have failed in this area in the past, and we want women in particular to feel protected and cherished here at IDC.

If you want to speak to a pastor at any time, we encourage you to do so.

This statement was not intended to be exhaustive but reflective of some basic principles regarding biblical teaching on the subject. To create culture as a pastoral leader, I recommend "the drip method of communication"—that is, regularly drip the vision of the church to people. Don't just have a once-a-year "Vision Sunday" where you blast the congregation with a fire hose! People should hear what we care about regularly (through sermon application, our pastoral prayers, and other public statements).

There are many things that we should drip (or emphasize), but I would especially encourage church leaders to drip this matter of caring for the abused as you consider it in light of the Great Commandment (particularly if your church sees a lot of turnover in attendance and membership). Let's create a culture that cares for the broken and bruised and point them to the Savior who heals and restores and renews.

Bibliography

Akin, Daniel L., ed, *A Theology for the Church*. Revised edition. Nashville: B&H, 2014.

Cole, R.A. *Galatians: An Introduction and Commentary*. Downers Grove, IL: InterVarsity Press, 1989.

Deese, Kaelan. "Divorces skyrocket in China amid lockdown." Article available at https://thehill.com/homenews/news /490564-divorces-skyrocket-in-china-amid-lockdown. Accessed May 1, 2020.

Gadsby, William. "Immortal Honors Rest on Jesus' Head." Lyrics online at https://hymnary.org/text/immortal_honors _rest_on_jesus_head. Accessed May 4, 2020.

Garland, David. *Colossians and Philemon*. The NIV Application Commentary. Grand Rapids: Zondervan, 1998.

George, Timothy, and John Woodbridge. *The Mark of Jesus.* Chicago: Moody, 2005.

Harvey, Dave. *When Sinners Say "I Do."* Wapwallopen, PA: Shepherd Press, 2007.

Jones, Robert D. *Uprooting Anger.* Phillipsburg, NJ: P&R, 2005.

Kempis, Thomas à. *The Inner Life.* New York: Penguin, 1952.

Kimble, Jeremy. *40 Questions about Church Membership and Discipline.* Grand Rapids: Kregel, 2017.

Moo, Douglas J. *The Letter of James.* Grand Rapids: Eerdmans, 2000.

Ortlund, Dane C. *Edwards on the Christian Life.* Wheaton: Crossway, 2014.

Piper, John. "Give God Your Revenge." Devotional available at https://www.desiringgod.org/articles/give-god-your-revenge. Accessed May 4, 2020.

Plantinga, Jr., Cornelius. *Not the Way It's Supposed to Be.* Grand Rapids: Eerdmans, 1995.

Poirier, Alfred J. "The Cross and Criticism." Article available at https://www.thegospelcoalition.org/article/cross-criticism/. Accessed April 28, 2020.

———. *The Peacemaking Pastor.* Grand Rapids: Baker, 2006.

Powlison, David. "Powlison on Lusts of the Flesh." An interview with Justin Taylor at https://www.thegospelcoalition.org /blogs/justin-taylor/powlison-on-lusts-of-flesh-question-4/. Accessed April 24, 2020.

Quarles, Charles. *Sermon on the Mount*. Nashville: B&H, 2011.

Rainer, Thom S. "Twenty Five Silly Things Church Members Fight Over." Article available at https://thomrainer.com /2015/11/twenty-five-silly-things-church-members-fight -over/. Accessed April 28, 2020.

Sande, Corlette. *The Young Peacemaker*. Wapwallopen, PA: Shepherd Press, 1997.

Sande, Ken. *The Peacemaker*. Grand Rapids: Baker, 2004.

Watson, Thomas. *The Doctrine of Repentance*. Reprint. Carlisle, PA: The Banner of Truth Trust, 2002.

Wright, N. T. *Colossians and Philemon*. Tyndale New Testament Commentaries. Grand Rapids: Eerdmans, 1986.